BIBLE™
DEFINITIONS

RON RHODES

HARVEST HOUSE PUBLISHERS

EUGENE, OREGON

Cover by Dugan Design Group, Bloomington, Minnesota

BITE-SIZE BIBLE™ DEFINITIONS
Copyright © 2011 by Ron Rhodes
Published by Harvest House Publishers
Eugene, Oregon 97402
www.harvesthousepublishers.com

ISBN 978-0-7369-3729-0 (Trade)
ISBN 978-0-7369-4121-1 (eBook)

Printed in the United States of America

11 12 13 14 15 16 17 / BP-NI / 10 9 8 7 6 5 4 3 2 1

To all who seek to be "doers of the word,
and not merely hearers who delude themselves"

(James 1:22)

Acknowledgments

I want to give a heartfelt thanks to the team at Harvest House Publishers for their continued commitment to excellence in Christian publishing. And as always, a big hug goes to my wife, Kerri, and our two children, David and Kylie, for their never-ending love and support.

What a tremendous gift God has given us in the Bible!

The word *Bible* means "book." The Bible is God's book for us. It's much like a manufacturer's handbook that instructs us how to operate our lives (2 Timothy 3:15-17).

The Bible is also like a pair of eyeglasses. Without the eyeglasses, we don't see clearly. But with the eyeglasses, all comes into clear focus (Psalm 119:18).

The Bible is also like a lamp. It sheds light on our path and helps us to see our way clearly (see Psalm 119:105).

The Bible is also like an anchor. Just as an anchor keeps a boat from floating away, so the Bible is an anchor for us. It prevents us from being swept away when a tidal wave of adversity comes our way (Hebrews 6:17-19).

The Bible is also like food (Matthew 4:4). It gives us spiritual nourishment. If we don't feed on God's Word, we become spiritually malnourished.

Lastly, the Bible is like a love letter or Valentine card from God to us. It reveals God's great love for us, which motivated Him to send Jesus into the world to die for our sins so we could be saved (John 3:16-17).

I've written *Bite-Size Bible Definitions* to help you better understand the Bible. With most of the Bible terms in the book, I've included Scripture references that contain broad information that illuminates the meaning of the terms, without necessarily mentioning the terms themselves. Such references are not intended to provide precise definitions (the Bible was not written as a dictionary). Instead, the verses will further your understanding of the terms by providing examples of how the Bible authors used them in different contexts.

I most commonly include terms as they appear in the New American Standard Bible (NASB), but as you'll see, occasionally the most familiar version of the term appears in the New International Version (NIV), English Standard Version (ESV), King James Version (KJV), or New King James Version (NKJV) instead.

In some instances, I've included the literal meaning of a term in parentheses immediately after the term, like this:

> **Adonijah** (Yahweh is my Lord): the fourth son of David (2 Samuel 3:4).

May this brief resource increase your understanding of—and excitement about—the Word of God!

Bite-Size Bible™ Definitions

Aaron: Moses' older brother and spokesman (Exodus 7:1-2,7-10,19). Aaron and his two sons are the forerunners of the Israelites' Aaronic priesthood (Exodus 24:1; Leviticus 8–9). Aaron was from the tribe of Levi, and the Levites were set apart for priestly and religious duties. Aaron had a lapse in judgment when he participated in molding a golden calf (Exodus 32).

Abaddon: the place of the dead (Job 26:6 NIV). Also, a destroyer angel of the bottomless pit (Revelation 9:11 NKJV).

Abba: a term of endearment, akin to "daddy" or "papa" (Mark 14:36; Romans 8:15).

Abednego: the Chaldee name given to Azariah, one of Daniel's companions (Daniel 1:7; 2:17) who was delivered from a burning furnace after refusing to worship an idol (3:12-30).

Abel: the second son of Adam and Eve, who was both righteous and full of faith (Hebrews 11:4). Cain, his older brother, murdered him because God accepted Abel's sacrifice but not Cain's (Genesis 4:1-16; Matthew 23:35). Abel gave not only the firstborn of his flock, but even the choicest of the firstborn.

Abimelech: the Philistine king of Gerar in the time of Abraham (Genesis 20:1-18). Also, the son of Abiathar, a high priest in the time of David (1 Chronicles 18:16).

Abiram: a son of Eliab who joined Korah in opposing Moses and Aaron. He and the other conspirators were swallowed up by an earthquake (Numbers 16:1-33; 26:9-10; Psalm 106:17).

Abner: King Saul's uncle and the commander of his army (1 Samuel 14:50; 17:55; 20:25). He became loyal to David (2 Samuel 3:12-13), and David mourned for him after Joab killed him (2 Samuel 3:33-38).

Abomination: something that is detested, often because of idolatry (Isaiah 44:19; 66:3; Ezekiel 22:11; Daniel 11:31; Matthew 24:15; Revelation 17:4).

Abomination of Desolation: a barbaric act of idolatry in which the antichrist will desecrate the Jewish temple by setting up an image of himself in it (Daniel 9:27; 11:31; 12:11; Matthew 24:15).

Abraham (father of a multitude): a patriarch who lived around 2000 BC. He originated from the city of Ur, in Mesopotamia, on the River Euphrates. God called him to leave Ur and go to the land of Canaan (Genesis 12:1). Abraham left with his wife, Sarah, and his nephew, Lot. Upon arriving in Canaan, his first act was to construct an altar to worship God. Abraham is an important ancestor of Jesus Christ (Matthew 1:1) and the father of all the faithful (Romans 4:16).

Abraham's Bosom: a metaphorical description of heaven, paradise, or the presence of God (Luke 16:23).

Abrahamic Covenant: God's promise that Abraham's descendants would be as numerous as the stars in the sky (Genesis 12:1-3; 13:14-17; 15:5). The promise may have seemed unbelievable to Abraham because his wife was childless (11:30). Yet Abraham did not doubt God; he knew God would faithfully give what He had promised. God reaffirmed the covenant in Genesis 15, perhaps to emphasize to Abraham that even in his advanced age, the promise would come to pass. God also promised Abraham that he would be personally blessed, that his name would become great, that those who bless him would be blessed and those who curse him would be cursed, and that all the families of the earth would be blessed through his posterity.

Absalom: a son of King David (2 Samuel 3:3) who rebelled against him and almost succeeded in usurping his throne (18:33).

Abyss: the abode of imprisoned demons or disobedient spirits (Revelation 9:1-21).

Achan: a man from the tribe of Judah who disobeyed God's command by taking plunder at the conquest of

Jericho. This crime resulted in the Israelites' defeat at Ai. Achan was promptly executed for his offense (Joshua 7).

Acts: part two of Luke's Gospel. The first book contains an orderly account of Jesus' accomplishments during His earthly life, and the book of Acts contains Luke's orderly account of Jesus' accomplishments through the Holy Spirit in the 30 years following Jesus' resurrection and ascension. It begins with Jesus' ascension into heaven and ends with the apostle Paul's imprisonment in Rome, linking the four Gospels to the epistles. Though the book of Acts may appear to focus on the acts of the apostles (primarily Paul and Peter), in reality it predominantly focuses on the acts of the Holy Spirit through these and other people.

Adam: the first human, who is also representative of the entire human race. His name is derived from a Hebrew word meaning "humanity" (Genesis 1:26-27; 2:7, 22-23). The Hebrew word for Eve (Adam's wife) means "giver of life," which is appropriate because the rest of humanity was born through her body. Genesis 2:21-22 contains a Hebrew play on words. *Man* in Hebrew is *ish*, and *woman* is *ishshah*. The name indicates that woman has the same nature as man (*ish*) but is different in some way (*shah*). The woman is a perfect companion of the opposite gender for man.

Adonai (Lord, Master): God. The name conveys God's absolute authority over humankind and the entire universe (Genesis 18:27).

Adonijah (Yahweh is my Lord): the fourth son of David (2 Samuel 3:4), who tried to position himself on the throne when his father was dying (1 Kings 1:5-53). David, however, made Solomon king (1 Kings 1:32-53).

Adoption: human adoptions (Exodus 2:10; Esther 2:7), God's adoption of Israel (Exodus 4:22; Deuteronomy 7:6; Hosea 11:1; Romans 9:4), and God's adoption of all believers into His eternal family, making them heirs who await their future inheritance in heaven (Romans 8:17, 23; Philippians 3:21; James 2:5).

Advent (coming, arrival): the first advent is the Incarnation, or the first coming of Christ. The second advent will be the second coming of Christ at the end of the future tribulation period. This word is not in the Bible, but it helps describe biblical truth.

Advocate: one who pleads a case on behalf of another or helps another by defending or comforting. The word is used of the relationship of Holy Spirit (see the KJV in John 14:16; 15:26; and 16:7) and Jesus Christ (1 John 2:1) to believers.

Agrippa: a name used of both the grandson and the great-grandson of Herod the Great (Agrippa I and Agrippa II). Agrippa I became ruler of all Palestine, persecuted the early Christians, slew James, and imprisoned Peter (he is also called Herod in Acts 12:1-4,23). Agrippa II (Acts 25:13; 26:2,7) heard the apostle Paul's case in AD 59 (Acts 26).

Ahab: a wicked king of Israel who married the idolatrous Jezebel from Tyre (1 Kings 16:29-31; 2 Kings 8:18; 2 Chronicles 22:3; Micah 6:16).

Ahasuerus: the Hebrew name of several kings in Scripture, including the king of Persia who married Esther (Esther 1:1). He was also known by his Persian name, Xerxes.

Ahaz: a wicked and idolatrous king of Judah who worshipped false gods and rejected the counsel of Isaiah the prophet (2 Kings 16; 2 Chronicles 28).

Alabaster: a precious perfume used by a woman to anoint Jesus' head as He dined in the house of Simon the leper (Matthew 26:7; Mark 14:3; Luke 7:37).

Alexander: the name of several New Testament people, including a relative of Annas the high priest (Acts 4:6), a Jew in Ephesus who opposed Paul (Acts 19:33), and a coppersmith who promoted heresies regarding the resurrection (1 Timothy 1:20; 2 Timothy 4:14).

Alleluia or **Hallelujah** (praise Yahweh): an exclamation of praise (Psalm 111–113; 135; 146–150; Revelation 19:1-6).

Alms: charitable gifts. Hebrews 13:16 instructs us to do good and share with others. Jesus admonished us to give to the poor (Matthew 19:21; Luke 11:41; 12:33) and to give to those who ask (Matthew 5:42). We are to share food with the hungry (Isaiah 58:7,10), to share money generously (Romans 12:8), and to use money for good (1 Timothy

6:17-18). The early church certainly showed charity as an evidence of Christian love (Acts 9:36; Romans 12:13; Ephesians 4:28; 1 Timothy 6:18; Hebrews 13:16; 1 John 3:17-19). Jesus advises us to give to others secretly instead of trying to win other people's praise (Matthew 6:1-2).

Alpha and Omega: a title of Christ, indicating He is the all-powerful one of eternity past and eternity future, the eternal God who has always existed and who will always exist (Isaiah 44:6; 48:12; Revelation 22:12-13).

Altar: a table or raised area on which priests offered sacrifices.

Altar of Burnt Offering: an altar in front of the entrance to the tabernacle (Exodus 40:6) on which priests offered sacrifices by fire (Exodus 29:13-34; Leviticus 1:3-17).

Altar of Incense: a table inside the tabernacle or temple, smaller than the altar of burnt offering, where priests burned incense morning and evening while they tended to the lamp (Exodus 37:25-26).

Amalek: the son of Eliphaz and grandson of Esau (Genesis 36:12; 1 Chronicles 1:36).

Amalekites: a nomadic people from Arabia Petraea who often opposed and attacked Israel (Exodus 17:8-13; Numbers 14:45; Deuteronomy 25:18).

Amen (so be it, truly): an affirmation of agreement (Psalm 41:13; 72:19; 89:52; 1 Corinthians 14:16).

Amillennialism: the view that when Christ comes, eternity will begin with no prior literal thousand-year reign on earth. Amillennialists generally interpret prophetic verses related to the reign of Christ metaphorically and say they refer to Christ's present (spiritual) rule from heaven.

Ammonites: a Semitic nation that descended from Ben-ammi and often fought against Israel (Judges 3:13). They were closely associated with the Moabites (Judges 10:11; 2 Chronicles 20:1; Zephaniah 2:8).

Amnon: a weak-charactered son of David who defiled Tamar, his half-sister, and was murdered by Absalom as a result (2 Samuel 3:2; 13:28-29; 1 Chronicles 3:1).

Amon: the name of several people, including the governor of Samaria in the time of Ahab (1 Kings 22:26; 2 Chronicles 18:25) and the son of Manasseh who became the fourteenth king of Judah (Zephaniah 1:1). Also, an Egyptian god (Jeremiah 46:25).

Amorites: an ancient Semitic warlike people who inhabited Palestine and Syria (Genesis 15:16; Exodus 34:11; Deuteronomy 1:27).

Amos (burden bearer): an Old Testament prophet and the book he wrote in approximately 755 BC. The book addresses the social injustice of Israel and its neighbors (Amos 5:24). During his time the land was prosperous, and there were many rich people. Yet the rich did not aid those who were disadvantaged. Amos, the farmer who became a prophet, therefore prophesied that a day of judgment was coming and that destruction would be inevitable (7:1–9:10).

Amram: the father of Aaron, Miriam, and Moses (Exodus 6:18,20; Numbers 3:19; 26:59). He died in Egypt when he was 137 (Exodus 6:20).

Anak or **Anakim:** very tall people who lived in Canaan during Israel's conquest (Numbers 13:22-23; Deuteronomy 9:2). Goliath may have been from among them.

Ananias: a man in Jerusalem who conspired with his wife to deceive the church and was struck dead for putting the Holy Spirit to the test (Acts 5:5). Also refers to a Christian in Damascus who prayed for Paul and became his instructor (Acts 9:10), as well as the high priest when Paul was imprisoned in Jerusalem (Acts 23:2).

Ancient of Days: Yahweh, the God and divine Judge of the universe (Daniel 7:9-10,13,22). He is pictured with clothing as white as snow, hair like pure wool, a throne of fiery flames, and many thousands of angelic attendants.

Andrew: one of Jesus' 12 apostles who lived in Bethsaida in Galilee (John 1:44). He was the brother of Simon Peter (Matthew 4:18; 10:2).

Angels: ministering spirits created by God (Hebrews 1:14). They are incorporeal and invisible (Hebrews 1:14), they are localized beings (Daniel 9:21-23), they can appear as men (Genesis 18), they are powerful (Psalm 103:20) and holy (Job 5:1; 15:15; Psalm 89:7), and they are obedient to God (Psalm 103:20). They serve as God's messengers (Matthew 1), help believers at the moment of death (Luke 16:22), restrain evil (Genesis 18:22; 19:1,10-11), execute God's judgments (Acts 12:22-23), and guard God's people (Psalm 91:11).

Anna: an aged prophetess who saw Christ as an infant and witnessed Simeon's words of thanks to God for fulfilling a promise to allow him to see the entrance of the Messiah into the world (Luke 2:36-37).

Annas: a high priest in office during the time of John the Baptist (Luke 3:2). Jesus was brought before him following His arrest for brief questioning (John 18:12-13,19-23).

Anoint: to sprinkle oil on someone or something in a ritual. It was a common form of consecrating high priests (Exodus 29:29; Leviticus 4:3), sacred vessels (Exodus 30:26), kings (1 Samuel 16:13), and prophets (1 Kings 19:16). Also used of the Holy Spirit's presence with believers (1 John 2:20,27).

Antichrist: a "man of lawlessness" (2 Thessalonians 2:3,8) who will perform counterfeit signs and wonders and deceive many during the tribulation period (2 Thessalonians 2:9-10). This demon-inspired individual will rise to prominence during the tribulation and try to dominate the world, destroy the Jews, persecute believers, and set up his own kingdom (Revelation 13). He will speak arrogant and boastful words, glorifying himself (2 Thessalonians 2:4). People around the world will be forced to receive his mark, without which they cannot buy or sell (Revelation 13:16-17). But to receive this mark is to receive God's wrath. This beast will be defeated and destroyed by Jesus at His second coming (Revelation 19:11-16). *See also* Spirit of Antichrist.

Antioch: a city in Syria about 300 miles north of Jerusalem. This is where the followers of Christ were first called Christians.

Antiochus Epiphanes: a Syrian king who reigned in the second century BC and who desecrated the temple at Jerusalem by slaughtering a pig in it. He is an idolatrous prototype of the antichrist, who will set up an image of himself in the temple (Daniel 11:31).

Antipas: a common name in New Testament times. The most famous was Herod Antipas, the tetrarch of Galilee and Peraea during the time of Christ (Luke 23:7). He was frivolous, vain, and evil (Mark 8:15; Luke 3:19; 13:31-32), and he murdered John the Baptist (Matthew 14:1-12). Another Antipas was a faithful martyr (Revelation 2:13).

Apocalypse (unveiling): an alternate name for the book of Revelation (Revelation 1:1).

Apollos: an Alexandrian Jew who became well versed in the Scriptures and eloquently defended Christian truth (Acts 18:24).

Apollyon (destroyer): a ruler of demonic spirits (Revelation 9:11).

Apostasy (falling away): a determined, willful defection from or abandonment of the faith (1 Timothy 1:19-20; 2 Timothy 4:10; Hebrews 6:5-8; 10:26).

Apostles: chosen messengers of Jesus Christ, including specifically the 12 disciples Jesus sent out to spread the good news of the gospel (Matthew 10:2-4). Just as the prophets were God's representatives in Old Testament times, so the apostles were God's representatives in New Testament times. They were specially handpicked by the Lord or the Holy Spirit (Matthew 10:1-4; Acts 1:26). They were the special recipients of God's self-revelation and were aware that God was providing revelation through them (1 Corinthians 2:13; 1 Thessalonians 2:13; 1 John 1:1-3). They clearly recognized their special divine authority (1 Corinthians 7:10; 11:23). Ephesians 2:19-20 explains that God's household is "built upon the foundation of the apostles and prophets," whom Christ had previously promised to guide into all the truth (John 14:26; 15:27; 16:13). God attested to the truth of their words through signs and wonders (Acts 2:43; 3:3-11; 5:12; 9:32-42; 20:6-12).

Aquila: a tent maker who engaged in missionary work with his wife, Priscilla, and the apostle Paul (Acts 18:2,18,26).

Ararat: a mountainous area in eastern Turkey where

Noah's ark came to rest after the catastrophic flood subsided (Genesis 8:4).

Archangel: the prince and leader of God's angels (1 Thessalonians 4:16; Jude 1:9). The term archangel occurs just twice in the New Testament, and in both instances it is used in the singular and is preceded by *the* (1 Thessalonians 4:16; Jude 9). Some scholars conclude from this that the term is restricted to a single archangel—Michael. He is called a "chief prince" (Daniel 10:13) and "the great prince" (Daniel 12:1), and he leads the other angels (Revelation 12:7).

Archelaus: a son of Herod the Great who became a ruler of Judea and Samaria (Matthew 2:22).

Areopagus: a hill in Athens where the apostle Paul preached (Acts 17:19,22-31).

Ariel: one of the chief men sent by Ezra to procure Levites for the sanctuary (Ezra 8:16). Also, a metaphorical reference to Jerusalem (Isaiah 29:1-2,7).

Ark: the boat Noah built at God's command. In it, a remnant of humans (Noah and his family) and animals were preserved from a flood that engulfed the entire world as a judgment from God (see Genesis 6:14–9:18). The ark was large—about 450 feet long, 75 feet wide, and 45 feet high—with three stories, providing room for plenty of animals (Genesis 6:16).

Ark of the Covenant: a cabinet constructed from the

wood of an acacia tree (which grows in the Sinai desert) and coated with gold. Built by a talented craftsman named Bezalel (Exodus 37:1), it measured about 45 by 27 by 27 inches and had rings at the four corners, through which poles were inserted for carrying. The ark contained the two stone tablets of the law written by the finger of God on Mount Sinai, which were a continual reminder of the covenant between God and Israel (Exodus 25:16,21). It also contained a pot of manna, which symbolized the bread of God from heaven (Exodus 16:33). Aaron's rod was later placed in it as a witness to Israel of God's choice of the priesthood (Numbers 17:10). The ark symbolized God's presence (1 Samuel 4:3-22). It was kept in the holy of holies, the innermost shrine of the tabernacle and the temple (Exodus 26:33). The lid of the ark was known as the mercy seat, and on each annual Day of Atonement, the high priest sprinkled the blood of a sacrificial animal on it to symbolize the nation's repentance for the sins committed the previous year (Leviticus 23:27; Numbers 29:7).

Armageddon: an end-times war campaign during the tribulation that includes the assembling of the antichrist's allies (Psalm 2:1-6; Joel 3:9-11; Revelation 16:12-16), Babylon's destruction (Isaiah 13–14; Jeremiah 50–51; Zechariah 5:5-11; Revelation 17–18), Jerusalem's fall (Micah 4:11–5:1; Zechariah 12–14), the gathering of the antichrist's armies at Bozrah (Jeremiah 49:13-14), Israel's national regeneration (Psalm 79:1-13; Isaiah 64:1-12; Hosea 6:1-11; Joel

2:28-32; Zechariah 12:10; Romans 11:25-27), the second coming (Isaiah 34:1-7; Micah 2:12-13; Habakkuk 3:3), the horrific battle from Bozrah to the Valley of Jehoshaphat (Jeremiah 49:20-22; Joel 3:12-13; Zechariah 14:12-15), and Christ's appearance on the Mount of Olives (Joel 3:14-17; Zechariah 14:3-5; Matthew 24:29-31; Revelation 16:17-21; 19:11-21).

Artaxerxes: the name of several Persian kings, including one who obstructed the rebuilding of the temple (Ezra 4:7).

Asaph: a Levite who, like David, was a skilled musician and wrote some of the psalms (1 Chronicles 15:16-19).

Ashdod: a Philistine city between Gaza and Joppa that was home to the idol worship of Dagon (1 Samuel 5:5).

Asher: Jacob's eighth son (his second with Zilpah, Leah's handmaid—Genesis 30:13). Also, Asher's descendants, who became one of Israel's tribes, and the land they inherited (Genesis 35:26; 46:17; Exodus 1:4).

Ashtoreth: the pagan moon goddess of the Phoenicians. She is often associated with Baal (Judges 10:6; 1 Samuel 7:4; 12:10).

Assyria: a Semitic nation on the Tigris River in what is now northern Iraq. Assyria was wealthy, had strong trade agreements with other nations, and built many temples for its pagan gods. The nation had a long history of animosity against Israel (Jonah 3:6-10; 4:1-3).

Astrology: a form of divination that allegedly forecasts events on earth by observing and interpreting the relationships between planets, stars, the sun, and the moon. It is forbidden by God (Isaiah 47:13,15; Daniel 2:2,10).

Athens: the most famous of the Greek cities and the capital of the Greek state of Attica. It was brimming with beautiful temples and buildings. The apostle Paul delivered a powerful sermon to the Greek-speaking philosophers there during his second missionary tour (Acts 17:22-34).

Atonement: the act by which God restores a relationship of harmony and unity between Himself and sinful human beings. The biblical words for atonement are rich in meaning. The Old Testament Hebrew word is *kaphar* (to cover, expiate, wipe away, placate, or cancel). The key thought is to cover over in God's eyes or to wipe away. The New Testament Greek term is *hiloskomai* (to propitiate, expiate, or conciliate). It is used only twice in the New Testament. In the first, a penitent sinner asks God to "be merciful" to him, hearkening back to the Old Testament image where God met the sinner at the mercy seat when blood atonement was made for sins (Luke 18:13). In the second, we read that Jesus "had to be made like his brothers in every way, in order that he might become a merciful and faithful high priest in service to God, and that he might make atonement for the sins of the people" (Hebrews 2:17 NIV). The background for Christ's atonement at the cross was laid in the Old Testament sacrificial system where blood atonement of innocent animals was regularly required for sins (Leviticus 4:14-21). This sacrificial system pointed forward to Christ's once-for-all blood sacrifice for our sins (1 Corinthians 5:7).

Augustus: a title of the first Roman emperor, Octavian, during whose reign Christ was born (Luke 2:1).

= B

Baal-Zebub: the god of the Philistines at Ekron (2 Kings 1:2-3,16).

Baal (lord): the king of the pagan gods who supposedly controlled heaven and earth (Judges 2:11; 10:10; 1 Kings 18:18; Jeremiah 2:23; Hosea 2:17). Baal was considered the god of fertility, so Baal temples housed male and female prostitutes. Worshippers believed that by having sex with temple prostitutes, they could obtain from Baal the things they wanted in life. The Bible condemns such Baal worship in the strongest possible terms (1 Kings 15:12).

Babel (confusion): a tower that was apparently a pagan effort to observe and worship the heavens (Genesis 11:1-9). God intervened by confounding the builders and confusing their languages.

Babylon: an ancient and influential civilization situated on the banks of the Euphrates River and ruled by kings and priests (Genesis 10:10). It was a commercial and trade center of the ancient world. The Babylonians believed in many false gods and goddesses and were heavily involved in divination (Daniel 1:20; 2:2,10,27; 4:7; 5:7,11,15). As a world power, Babylon destroyed Jerusalem and took its people captive. Babylon is often represented in Scripture as opposing Yahweh and His people (2 Kings 24:10).

Balaam: a non-Israelite prophet whose false teaching encouraged such sins as idolatry and sexual immorality (Numbers 22–25; 31; Revelation 2:14).

Balak: a Moabite king who hired Balaam to hinder the Israelites from entering the Promised Land (Numbers 22:2,4).

Baptism: a ritual immersion in water pointing to a believer's complete identification with Jesus Christ. It is a public testimony that shouts to the world that a change in status has occurred in the person's life. Formerly, the person was identified with the world and was lost, but now the person is identified with Jesus Christ. The immersion into the water and the coming up out of it symbolizes death to the old life and resurrection to the new life in Christ (Romans 6:1-4).

Bar-Jesus: a Jewish false prophet and magician-sorcerer who encountered Paul and Barnabas at Paphos (Acts 13:6).

Barabbas: a robber and murderer whom Pilate tried to condemn to death so he could release Jesus (Mark 15:7; Luke 23:19; John 18:40).

Barak: the son of Abinoam (Judges 4:6) who led Israel in war against Jabin. Barak's faith is commended in Hebrews 11:32.

Barbarian (one who speaks an unintelligible language): commonly used in reference to non-Greeks (Romans 1:14; 1 Corinthians 14:11).

Barnabas (son of encouragement—Acts 4:36): an apostle with a good reputation (Acts 11:24). He accompanied the apostle Paul on his first missionary journey.

Bartholomew: one of the 12 apostles (Matthew 10:3; Acts 1:13).

Bathsheba: the beautiful daughter of Eliam and the wife of Uriah the Hittite. David committed adultery with her and had Uriah killed (2 Samuel 11:4-5; Psalm 51:1).

Beatitudes (blessings): the eight blessings Jesus pronounced at the beginning of the Sermon on the Mount (Matthew 5:1-12). The word *blessed* literally means "happy, fortunate, or blissful." Blessing involves a divinely bestowed sense of well-being, which constitutes a foretaste of heaven. In the beatitudes, then, Jesus depicts the means of a person attaining a divinely bestowed sense of well-being in daily life. True happiness is found in following Jesus' wisdom. The actual literary form of the beatitudes is rooted in wisdom literature, especially Psalms. Indeed, in Psalms we often find the words, "Blessed are..." (Psalm 2:12; 65:4; 84:4-5; 89:15; 106:3; 119:1).

Beelzebul or **Beelzebub** (lord of the flies): the devil (Matthew 12:24).

Beersheba: a well Abraham dug (Genesis 21:31). Also, a city given to the tribe of Simeon (Joshua 19:2; 1 Chronicles 4:28).

Behemoth: an unidentified large animal, perhaps a hippopotamus or even a dinosaur (Job 40:15).

Belial (worthlessness): Satan (2 Corinthians 6:15).

Belshazzar: the last king of Babylon (Daniel 5:1).

Belteshazzar: a Chaldee name given to the prophet Daniel when he was chosen to serve in Nebuchadnezzar's court in Babylon (Daniel 1:7).

Benjamin: Jacob's twelfth son (his second with Rachel—Genesis 35:18). Also, Benjamin's descendants, who became a tribe in Israel, and the land they inherited.

Berea: a Macedonian city near Mount Olympus. Paul, Silas, and Timothy preached there to Jews who received the word and examined the Scriptures daily (Acts 17:10-13).

Beth-Togarmah (house of Togarmah): a territory to the north of Israel in modern-day Turkey (Ezekiel 38:6).

Bethany: a small village on the southeastern side of the Mount of Olives (Mark 11:1). It was the hometown of Mary, Martha, and their brother Lazarus, whom Jesus raised from the dead (Matthew 21:17; 26:6; Mark 11:11-12; John 11:1-44).

Bethel (house of God): a city north of Jerusalem. It had previously been called Luz, but Jacob renamed it after receiving a vision of God there (Genesis 28:10-19). It eventually became a center of idolatry for the northern kingdom (1 Kings 12:25-33).

Bethesda: a pool, bath, or reservoir in Jerusalem that had five porches. Jesus healed a lame man there (John 5:2-9).

Bethlehem: a city in the hill country of Judah where David was born (hence the alternate name, city of David—Luke 2:4). Jesus Christ was also born there, fulfilling a 700-year-old prophecy (Micah 5:2; Matthew 2:1).

Bethsaida: a city on the northern shore of the Sea of Galilee where Peter, Andrew, and Philip lived (Matthew 11:21; Mark 6:45; 8:22; Luke 9:10; 10:13).

Betrothal: a binding commitment between a man and a woman that was stronger than engagement and often took place a year or more before marriage (Deuteronomy 28:30; Judges 14:2,8; Matthew 1:18-21).

Bildad: one of Job's well-meaning but misguided comforters (Job 2:11; 18:1; 42:9).

Bilhah: Rachel's servant, whom she gave to Jacob to bear children for her (Genesis 29:29). Bilhah was the mother of Dan and Naphtali (Genesis 30:3-8).

Birthright: the special privileges belonging to the first-born son in the family, including a double portion of the family inheritance (Deuteronomy 21:15-17).

Blasphemy: irreverence or contempt for God or for something considered sacred (Leviticus 24:16; Matthew 26:65; Mark 2:7).

Bless: to bestow favor on another. God blesses His people with temporal as well as spiritual gifts (Genesis 1:22; 24:35; Job 42:12; Psalm 45:2; 104:24,35). People bless God by giving thanks to Him (Psalm 103:1-2; 145:1-2). People bless one another by expressing good wishes or offering prayers on their behalf (Genesis 24:60; 31:55; 1 Samuel 2:20).

Blood: a central component in the biblical doctrine of atonement. In Leviticus 17:11, God said, "The life of a creature is in the blood, and I have given it to you to make atonement for yourselves on the altar; it is the blood that makes atonement for one's life." This points forward to the necessity of Christ's blood sacrifice in the New Testament. As Hebrews 9:22 (NIV) says, "The law requires that nearly everything be cleansed with blood, and without the shedding of blood there is no forgiveness." And nothing but the blood sacrifice of Jesus, the Lamb of God, could ultimately bring atonement for the sins of all humankind (John 1:29).

Boaz: a rich nobleman who married the widow Ruth (Ruth 4:1-13).

Book of Life: a heavenly book containing the names of the redeemed, who will inherit heaven (Luke 10:20; Philippians 4:3; Revelation 3:5; 13:8; 20:12,15; 21:27). The names of God's elect have been inscribed in this book "from the foundation of the world" (Revelation 17:8). The concept of a book of life apparently harkens back to Moses' request that God blot his name from God's book rather than dooming his fellow Israelites (Exodus 32:32-33). Psalm 69:28 refers to this same book. In the end times, those whose names are not found in God's book of life will be cast into the lake of fire (Revelation 20:15).

Book of the Wars of the Lord: an unknown ancient Hebrew book mentioned in the Bible (Numbers 21:14-15).

Born Again or **Born from Above:** having received eternal life, which God gives to those who believe in Christ (Titus 3:5). Just as a physical birth places a new baby into a family, so a spiritual birth places a believer into the family of God (John 3:1-5; 1 Peter 1:23).

Breastplate: armor designed to protect the chest during battle. Also, a figurative New Testament term for righteousness, part of the Christian's armor in spiritual warfare (Ephesians 6:14).

Brimstone: burning sulfur. Sodom and Gomorrah were destroyed by brimstone as a judgment from God (Genesis 19:24-25).

Brother: either a natural sibling (Matthew 1:2), a cousin (Genesis 13:8; 14:16), a disciple or follower (Matthew 25:40; Hebrews 2:11-12), a person of the same faith (Amos 1:9; Acts 9:30; 11:29; 1 Corinthians 5:11), or one's fellow man (Genesis 9:5; 19:7; Matthew 5:22-24).

Burnt Offering: a sacrifice that symbolizes homage and total dedication to God (Leviticus 6:22). Examples of burnt offerings include those of Abel (Genesis 4:3-4), Noah (Genesis 8:20), Abraham (Genesis 22:2,7-8,13), and the Hebrews in Egypt (Exodus 10:25).

C

Caesar: a title assumed by several Roman emperors following Julius Caesar (John 19:15; Acts 17:7).

Caesarea Philippi: a city near the base of Mount Hermon on the northern perimeter of Jesus' public ministry (Matthew 16:13; Mark 8:27).

Caesarea: a city on the shore of the Mediterranean, 70 miles northwest of Jerusalem, to the south of Mount Carmel. Cornelius converted to Christ there following an encounter with Peter (Acts 10:1,24).

Caiaphas: the Jewish high priest in office at the beginning of Jesus' public ministry. He also presided over one of

Jesus' trials (Matthew 26:3,57; John 11:49; 18:13-14). He was a member of the Sadducees (Acts 5:17).

Cain: the firstborn son of Adam and Eve (Genesis 4:1). This farmer murdered his brother Abel (1 John 3:12) and was consequently expelled and exiled from Eden (Genesis 4:10-15).

Caleb: one of the 12 spies Moses sent to survey the Promised Land (Numbers 13:6; 32:12; Joshua 14:6,14). Only he and Joshua encouraged the Israelites to go possess the land (Numbers 13–14).

Cana: a small town in Galilee near Nazareth. Jesus turned water into wine there (John 2:1-11; 4:46).

Canaan: the fourth son of Ham (Genesis 10:6). Also a name for the Promised Land—the entire country to the west of the Jordan and the Dead Sea (Deuteronomy 11:30). This is the land God promised to Abraham and his descendants (Genesis 12:1).

Canaanites: inhabitants of Canaan from about 2000 BC until the Israelites' conquest of that territory (recorded in the book of Joshua). The Canaanites' religion was polytheistic, but El was their most important deity.

Capernaum: a city located on the northwest shore of the Sea of Galilee where much of Jesus' public ministry transpired (Matthew 8:5,14-15; 9:2-6,10-17; 15:1-20; Mark 1:32-34).

Cappadocia: the largest province in Asia Minor. The gospel was preached there very early (1 Peter 1:1).

Captivity: specifically, the Israelites' exile as a result of their disobedience to God (Deuteronomy 28:15-68). The two most significant periods of Israelite captivity began with the fall of the northern kingdom (Israel) to the Assyrians in 722 BC and the collapse of the southern kingdom (Judah) to the Babylonians in 597–581 BC.

Carmel: a range of hills in central Palestine where Elijah slew the prophets of Baal (1 Kings 18). Also, a town in the hill country of Judah where King Uzziah grew his vineyards (2 Chronicles 26:10).

Carnal: of the flesh, worldly, sinful, unspiritual. This is the attitude and lifestyle of Christians who are not yet yielded to the Spirit of Christ (Romans 8:6-7; 1 Corinthians 3:3; 2 Corinthians 10:4 NKJV and KJV).

Censer: a pan used for burning incense in the temple (Numbers 16:17 KJV, NKJV, NIV).

Centurion: a Roman officer in command of a hundred soldiers (Mark 15:39,44-45). One centurion who witnessed the crucifixion of Jesus Christ exclaimed, "Truly this was the Son of God" (Mathew 27:54). Cornelius was a centurion who converted to Christ (Acts 10:1,22).

Cephas (stone): the Aramaic form of *Peter*, the name Christ gave to Simon following his confession of faith (Matthew 16:16-18; John 1:42).

Cereal Offering or **Grain Offering**: a sacrifice of thankfulness that produced "an aroma pleasing to the LORD." The priests burned a handful and ate the rest (Leviticus 2:1-3).

Chaff: unusable husks that separate from seed during the process of threshing grain (Exodus 15:7; Isaiah 5:24; Matthew 3:12). The term is sometimes metaphorically applied to wicked people (Psalm 1:4; Jeremiah 23:28; Matthew 3:12).

Chaldea: a territory in southern Babylon (Jeremiah 50:10; 51:24,35).

Chemosh: a Moabite fish-deity that was worshipped with human sacrifice (Numbers 21:29; Jeremiah 48:7,13,46).

Cherubim: powerful, majestic, and indescribably beautiful angels of the highest order who surround God's throne and defend His holiness from contamination by sin (Genesis 3:24; Exodus 25:18,20; Ezekiel 1:1-18; 28:12-13,17). They guarded Eden after the expulsion of Adam and Eve (Genesis 3:24). Figures of cherubim adorned the ark of the covenant, positioned in such a way that they gaze upon the mercy seat (Exodus 25:17-22). Cherubim also adorned Solomon's temple (1 Kings 6:23-28). They were represented on the veil that barred the entrance to the holy of holies. The Old Testament pictures God descending to the earth on a cherub (2 Samuel 22:11; Psalm 18:10).

Chosen People: this term is not in the Bible, but it is a helpful description of the Jews (Exodus 19:4-6; Deuteronomy 7:6,8; Psalm 105:43), not only because the divine Messiah would be born a Jew (Genesis 12:1-3; 2 Samuel 12:13-14; Matthew 1:1) but also because God chose the Jews to present Him to all the nations of the earth. They were to be a light to the Gentiles (Isaiah 42:6). Though the Jews failed at this task (they did not even recognize the true Messiah), many Bible expositors believe the 144,000 Jews mentioned in Revelation 7 and 14 will, in the end times, finally fulfill the task to which the Jewish nation was called—they will indeed be a light to the entire world, sharing the truth of Jesus Christ.

Christians: those belonging to Christ (Acts 11:26; 26:28; 1 Peter 4:16). The word is used only three times in the New Testament, most importantly in Acts 11:26 (*see also* Acts 26:28; 1 Peter 4:16). In Acts 11:26, we are told simply and straightforwardly, "The disciples were first called Christians at Antioch." This would have been around AD 42, about a decade after Christ died on the cross and was resurrected from the dead.

Chronicles, 1 and **2:** books written by an unidentified author between 450 and 425 BC. They draw most of their information from the books of Samuel and Kings, covering the time of the judges to the exile. They emphasize that Israel is blessed by God when it is obedient, but it is punished by Him when it is disobedient. The material is essentially the same as in the books of Samuel and Kings, but it is presented from the vantage point of Jewish exiles returning from Babylon to Jerusalem.

Church: the ever-enlarging body of born-again believers who comprise the universal body of Christ, over whom He reigns as Lord. Although the members of the church differ in age, sex, race, wealth, social status, and ability, they are all joined together as one people (Galatians 3:28). All of them share in one Spirit and worship one Lord (Ephesians 4:3-6). This body is comprised only of believers in Christ. People become members of this universal body by simply placing their faith in Christ. The word *church* is translated from the Greek word *ekklesia*. This Greek word comes from two smaller words, *ek* (out from among) and *klesia* (to call). Combining the two words, *ekklesia* means "to call out from among." The church represents those whom God has called out from all walks of life. All are welcome in Christ's church.

Circumcision: the Jewish ritual of cutting away the foreskin of the male organ (Exodus 4:25; Joshua 5:2). It was a sign of the covenant God made with Abraham (Genesis 15).

Cistern: a large reservoir cut from stone or clay that collected and stored rainwater (2 Kings 18:31).

City of David: Bethlehem (Luke 2:4,11), where King David and Jesus Christ, the Son of David, were born.

Cities of Refuge: six cities to which Israelites accused of a crime could flee for asylum (Numbers 35).

Clean and **Unclean**: terms used in reference to ritual defilement. Things that rendered one unclean include a woman's menstruation (Leviticus 12:2-5; Ezekiel 16:4) and touching a dead animal (Leviticus 11:24-40). Unclean people could be restored through purification rituals prescribed by the Mosaic Law.

Colossae: a city of Phrygia in Asia Minor. Paul wrote a letter to the church in this city (Colossians 1:2).

Colossians: the apostle Paul's letter to the Christians in Colossae, written in AD 61 to help correct a tendency to mix Christianity with other philosophies and religions. The church in Colossae included both Greeks and Jews, and some of them—especially the Jews—appear to have incorporated some distinctly unchristian religious ideas into Christianity, including Jewish food laws and festivals (Colossians 2:16), circumcision (2:11), mysticism (2:18), and an over-elevated view of angels (2:18). They were also ultimately teaching that without such ideas, Christianity was incomplete. This was unsettling to Paul, and he sought to correct such ideas in this epistle.

Comforter (one who consoles): the Holy Spirit (see the KJV in John 14:16,26; 15:26; 16:7).

Concubine: a woman who lives with a man but is not married to him (Genesis 22:24) or a woman in a king's harem (1 Kings 11:3; Esther 2:12-14). Israelite law provided for the protection of concubines (Exodus 21:7), though they had no real authority in the family.

Confession: a profession of faith (Luke 12:8) or an acknowledgment of sins (Leviticus 16:21; Ezra 9:5-15; Daniel 9:3-12; 1 John 1:9).

Congregation (assembly): the collective community of Israelites in Old Testament times (Exodus 12:3).

Conscience: an inborn sense of right and wrong. Believers are exhorted to keep a good conscience (Acts 24:16; Romans 9:1; 2 Corinthians 1:12; 1 Timothy 1:5,19; 1 Peter 3:21) because a conscience can be seared (1 Timothy 4:1-3).

Consecration: the act of dedicating a person or a thing to the Lord (Exodus 19:22-23; 29:33).

Consolation of Israel: the Messiah (Luke 2:25).

Conversion: the turning of a soul, by divine grace, from sin to God (Acts 15:3).

Corban: irrevocably dedicated and consecrated to God or the temple. Jesus condemned Pharisees who did not support their parents financially because their earthly goods were Corban (Mark 7:11).

Corinth: a Grecian city on the northern shore of Peloponnesus, about 48 miles west of Athens. Its mixed population of Romans, Greeks, and Jews was notorious for immorality. As a hub of commerce with a mixed population, Corinth was a strategic city for the spread of the gospel. Paul wrote two epistles to the church in this city.

Corinthians, 1 and **2**: two letters from the apostle Paul. He wrote the first in AD 55 to correct such problems in the Corinthian church as schisms (1 Corinthians 1–4), moral issues, Christians and litigation, food sacrificed to idols, payment for those involved in ministry, distinctive ministries of men and women, the Lord's Supper, charismatic gifts, and the resurrection from the dead (1 Corinthians 5–15).

Paul wrote his second letter to the Corinthians in AD 56 to defend his ministry and his God-given authority as an apostle of God. Apparently, false prophets had penetrated the Corinthian church and assaulted Paul's character and authority. Some of the Corinthians had apparently believed their lies and rebelled against Paul. These false teachers were leading the people astray, and unless Paul acted decisively, the entire church might become engulfed in demonic doctrines. Paul thus intervened and made a "painful visit" to them (2 Corinthians 2:1 ESV, NIV). He followed up this visit with a "severe letter," which is no longer in our possession (2:4). Later, Titus was able to pass on news to Paul that the majority of Corinthian believers had repented of their rebellion against him (7:7). Grieved at past strained relations, Paul sought to clarify his ministry and his calling and authority as an apostle and to bring unity to the church. It is clear from what he wrote that he had a strong love for the Corinthian believers. He sought to see them grow spiritually.

Cornelius: a Roman centurion who converted to Christ after Peter explained the gospel to him (Acts 10).

Covenant: treaties or alliances between nations (1 Samuel 11:1) or individuals (Genesis 21:27). Also, friendship pacts (1 Samuel 18:3-4) and, most importantly, agreements between God and His people (Genesis 9:8-17; 15:12-21; 17:1-14; Exodus 19:5-6; 2 Samuel 7:13; 23:5; Jeremiah 31:31; Hebrews 8:6-13).

Creation: God's action of bringing all things in the universe into being (Genesis 1:1; Psalm 96:5; Isaiah 37:16; 44:24; 45:12; Jeremiah 10:11-12). God created the universe *ex nihilo* (out of nothing) instantaneously (Psalm 33:6,9).

Crown: a king's diadem (2 Samuel 1:10; 2 Kings 11:12) or a symbol of victory and reward. Spiritually, crowns are the rewards believers will receive or lose at the judgment seat of Christ (Romans 14:8-10; 1 Corinthians 9:25; 2 Timothy 4:8; James 1:12; 1 Peter 5:4; 2 John 8; Revelation 2:10).

Crucifixion: a particularly cruel Roman mode of execution. The Old Testament predicted Jesus' crucifixion several centuries before crucifixion even existed (Psalm 22:14-18,24; 34:20; 69:21; Isaiah 53:5,12; Zechariah 12:10).

Cubit: a linear unit of measure that was roughly the length of a person's forearm (18 to 20 inches).

Cupbearer: a high-ranking and trusted government official who ensured that the king's wine was not poisoned (Genesis 40:1-21; 41:9).

Curse: a verbal condemnation. God pronounced certain curses (Genesis 3:14; 4:11), as did some of God's spokesmen (Genesis 9:25; 49:7; Deuteronomy 27:15; Joshua 6:26).

Cush: the territory just south of Egypt on the Nile River in modern-day Sudan (Ezekiel 38:5 NIV).

Cyprus: a large island in the Mediterranean about 60 miles from the Syrian coast (Numbers 24:24 NKJV).

Cyrus: the king of Persia who conquered Babylon and issued a decree for the liberation of the Jews, allowing them to return to Jerusalem and rebuild their temple (Ezra 1:1-2; Isaiah 44:28).

D

Dagon: the principle pagan deity of the Philistines, whose image was the body of a fish with the head and hands of a man (Judges 16:23).

Damascus: the capital city of Syria, about 133 miles north of Jerusalem (see Isaiah 7:8; 17:3).

Dan: Jacob's fifth son (his first with Bilhah, Rachel's servant—Genesis 30:6). Also, Dan's descendants, who became one of Israel's tribes, and the land they inherited (Joshua 19:40-48).

Daniel: a Jewish youth deported to Babylon along with many other Jews as a result of Nebuchadnezzar's siege of Jerusalem in 605 BC. In Babylon Daniel rose to a position of prominence through his commitment to God and the skills God had given him. Daniel was famously rescued from a lion's den (Daniel 6).

Also, the apocalyptic book he wrote in approximately 537 BC. It emphasizes God's control over all human events. It also stresses that even though God's people were suffering great persecution in their exile in Babylon, God was nevertheless in control and had not abandoned them. He would eventually deal with Israel's oppressors and set Israel free (Daniel 12).

Darius: a popular name among Persian kings, most famously used in reference to Darius the Mede (Daniel 11:1), under whose reign Daniel was promoted to high authority and dignity (6:1-2). Darius was tricked into throwing Daniel into a den of lions. After Daniel survived a dangerous night by a miraculous angelic deliverance, however, Darius issued a decree enjoining reverence for the God of Daniel (6:26).

David: the last of eight children born to Jesse. David became instantly famous for killing Goliath, the giant Philistine warrior (1 Samuel 17). He was also a gifted musician (1 Samuel 16:18-23). When David was a shepherd, God unexpectedly chose him to become Israel's second king, although he was not crowned until he was 30 years old

(2 Samuel 2:1-7) following Saul's death. He made Jerusalem his capital and ruled for 40 years (1 Samuel 16–31; 2 Samuel 1–24; 1 Kings 1–2; and 1 Chronicles 10–29). In his old age, David made his son Solomon king in his place. He died at 71 in his own bed.

Davidic Covenant: a term Bible scholars use to describe the covenant God made with David in which He promised that one of David's descendants would rule forever (2 Samuel 7:12-13; 22:51). This is an example of an unconditional covenant. It did not depend on David in any way for its fulfillment. David realized this when he received the promise from God, and he responded with humility and a recognition of God's sovereignty over the affairs of men. This covenant finds its ultimate fulfillment in Jesus Christ, who was born from the line of David (Matthew 1:1).

Day of Atonement: an annual Israelite celebration on the tenth day of the seventh month of the Jewish calendar. The high priest entered into the holy of holies to offer a sacrifice of atonement—first for his own sins and then for the sins of the people (see Leviticus 4:5; 16; 23:27; Hebrews 9:9; 10:24). These sacrifices took place annually, so the Israelites were reminded every year that their sin cut them off from God and regularly required atonement. This makes the sacrifice of Christ all the more important, for His sacrifice was once and for all, never again to be repeated (Hebrews 9:9; 10:24).

Day of the Lord: In the Old Testament, this was a

God-ordained event (often involving judgment) to be fulfilled in the near future or in the distant eschatological future. In the New Testament, it is the judgment that will climax in the future seven-year tribulation period (2 Thessalonians 2:2; Revelation 16–18).

Deacon (servant): a person who helps to meet church members' material needs (Acts 6:1-6; 1 Timothy 3:8-12).

Dead Sea: a sea to the east of Jerusalem with an area of about 300 square miles. It is also known as the Salt Sea (Genesis 14:3; Numbers 34:12), the Sea of the Plain (Deuteronomy 3:17 KJV), and the East Sea (Ezekiel 47:18; Joel 2:20).

Death: The Old Testament concept is of separation (for example, man's separation from God). This is continued in the New Testament, which teaches that at death, the Christian's spirit immediately separates from the body to be with the Lord (2 Corinthians 5:8). Death for the believer is thus an event that leads to a supremely blissful existence (Philippians 1:21). For the unbeliever, however, death holds grim prospects. At death the unbeliever's spirit departs from the body and goes not to heaven, but to a place of great suffering (Luke 16:19-31). Both believers and unbelievers remain as disembodied spirits until the future day of resurrection. Believers' resurrection bodies will be specially suited to dwelling in heaven in the direct presence of God—the perishable will be made imperishable and the mortal will be made immortal (1 Corinthians

15:53). Unbelievers will also be resurrected, but they will spend eternity apart from God (John 5:29).

Deborah: the name of several biblical persons, including Rebekah's nurse (Genesis 35:8) and a highly respected prophetess (Judges 4:6,14; 5:7).

Decapolis (ten cities): a confederation on the east-southeast side of the Sea of Galilee containing ten cities inhabited by Greeks (Matthew 4:25; Mark 5:20; 7:31): Scythopolis, Hippos, Gadara, Pella, Philadelphia, Gerasa, Dion, Canatha, Raphana, and Damascus.

Decree: a ruler's order or declaration. Royal decrees were common in biblical times (Ezra 4:19,21; 5:3,9,13).

Delilah: a beautiful Philistine woman with whom Samson fell in love. Philistine leaders bribed her to entice Samson to reveal the secret of his strength and the means of overcoming it (Judges 16:4-20).

Demons: angels who sided with Lucifer in his rebellion against God and who continue to be aligned against God and His people (Isaiah 14:12-15; Ezekiel 28:12-19; Revelation 12:7). Scripture portrays demons as evil and wicked. They are designated "unclean spirits" (Matthew 10:1 KJV, NKJV), "evil spirits" (Luke 7:21), and "spiritual forces of wickedness" (Ephesians 6:12). All these terms point to demons' immoral nature. Under Satan's lead, they seek to disseminate false doctrine (1 Timothy 4:1) through false prophets (1 John 4:1-4) and to turn men to the worship of idols

(Leviticus 17:7; Deuteronomy 32:17; Psalm 106:36-38). Demons hinder answers to the believers' prayers (Daniel 10:12-20) and instigate jealousy and faction among believers (James 3:13-16). Demons inflict physical diseases on people, such as dumbness, blindness, and epilepsy (Matthew 9:33; 12:22; 17:15-18). They also afflict people with mental disorders (Mark 5:4-5; 9:22; Luke 8:27-29; 9:37-42). They cause people to be self-destructive (Mark 5:5; Luke 9:42). They are even responsible for some deaths (Revelation 9:14-19).

Deuteronomy (second law): a book written by Moses in about 1410 BC that contains the words Moses spoke to the Israelites as they were camped in the plains of Moab, preparing to enter into the Promised Land (Deuteronomy 1:1). This was Moses' farewell address; his protégé, Joshua, succeeded him. The book contains a restatement and reaffirmation of the covenant God made with the Israelites at Sinai. It also recounts many of the laws. For example, the Ten Commandments recorded in Exodus 20 are repeated in Deuteronomy 5 with minor variations.

Devil (adversary, slanderer): the adversary of Christ and all who follow Christ. Satan slanders God to man (Genesis 3:1-7), and man to God (Job 1:9; 2:4).

Diadem: a crown (Ezekiel 21:26; Isaiah 28:5; 62:3).

Diotrephes: a prideful, self-loving Judaizer who persecuted believers (3 John 1:9).

Disciple (learner): specifically, one of the 12 men Jesus chose to be His apostles (Mark 3:13-19; Luke 6:13). These men spent three years with Him, digesting His teachings and witnessing His mighty miracles among the people. Later, these disciples were called apostles (Luke 6:13). They included Peter, Andrew, James, John, Philip, Bartholomew, Thomas, Nathaniel, Matthew, and others. In a more general sense, the term refers to all who follow Christ (Matthew 16:24; Luke 14:33; John 8:31; 15:8).

Divination: occult practice intended to determine the future or the will of the gods. It includes spiritism (Deuteronomy 18:11; 1 Samuel 28:3,9), witchcraft (Numbers 22:7; 23:23; Joshua 13:22), and conjuring spells (Deuteronomy 18:11). The Bible condemns all forms of occultism (Leviticus 19:26).

Divorce: the dissolution of a marriage, allowable only under two circumstances: unfaithfulness (Matthew 19:9) and desertion by an unbelieving partner (1 Corinthians 7:15-16).

Dominions: an order of angels (Colossians 1:16).

Dowry: a bridegroom's financial payment to the father of the bride (Genesis 34:12; Exodus 22:17; 1 Samuel 18:25).

Dragon: a metaphorical reference to Satan (Revelation 20:2).

Drink Offering: a liquid (such as wine) poured out in a ritual of worship to God (Exodus 29:40).

== **E**

Earnest: a pledge of something to come. The Holy Spirit is the earnest of the believer's heavenly inheritance (2 Corinthians 1:22 KJV; 5:5; Ephesians 1:14 KJV).

Earth: soil (Genesis 9:20 KJV), the whole world (Genesis 1:2), land as opposed to sea (Genesis 1:10), or the ground on which a man stands (Genesis 33:3).

Ecclesiastes: a book apparently written by Solomon in 935 BC that presents two contrasting viewpoints. One is the secular, humanistic, materialistic view of all things from a limited earthly perspective—a perspective "under the sun" that does not recognize God or His involvement in human affairs (Ecclesiastes 1:14; 2:11,17,26; 4:4,16; 6:9). This earthly perspective is unaided by divine revelation. In it, life is futile, without meaning and purpose.

The other perspective is spiritual and interprets life and its problems from a God-honoring viewpoint (3:1-15; 5:19; 6:1-2; 9:1). This perspective recognizes God and interprets life and its problems according to divine revelation. It finds meaning, purpose, and joy in life. God can be involved in all that we do (2:24-26; 3:13; 5:18-20; 9:7-10).

Eden (delight): the garden of splendor where God placed our first parents, Adam and Eve (Genesis 2:8-17).

Edom: Esau, Isaac and Rebekah's firstborn twin son, who

was characterized by being hairy (Genesis 25:25). Also, his descendants and the land they inhabited (Genesis 36:16; Numbers 20:14-21).

Egypt: a country at the northeast corner of Africa that naturally divides into two realms—Upper Egypt, which is the valley of the Nile, and Lower Egypt, which is the plain of the Delta. Egypt worshipped more than 80 deities. The book of Exodus describes God's deliverance of the Israelites from Egyptian slavery.

El Shaddai: God (Genesis 17:1-20). The Hebrew word *El* means "Mighty God." But *Shaddai* derives from a root word that refers to a mother's breast. This name, then, indicates not only that God is Mighty but also that He is the provider who is full of compassion, grace, and mercy.

Elder: a person in authority and worthy of respect. Elders were recognized in Old Testament Israel (Exodus 3:16; 24:1; Numbers 11:16-17) and in the New Testament church (Acts 20:17-28; Ephesians 4:11; Philippians 1:1; 1 Thessalonians 5:12; Titus 1:5-7; Hebrews 13:7). God provides elders who can protect His people from doctrinal and moral error.

Eli: a high priest (1 Samuel 1:3,9) and judge of Israel (1 Samuel 4:18). His sons Hophni and Phinehas engaged in gross misconduct (1 Samuel 2:27-36), and because Eli failed to reprove them, God's judgment fell on his house (1 Samuel 2:22-33; 3:18).

Elihu: the name of several biblical persons, the most famous being one of Job's well-meaning but misguided comforters (Job 32–37).

Elijah (the Lord is my God): an animated prophet who dressed strangely and lived an ascetic lifestyle (2 Kings 1:8) while ministering during Ahab's and Ahaziah's reigns in the northern kingdom (Israel) in the ninth century BC. He is well known for defending faithful obedience to the one true God of Israel, as he did when he challenged and defeated the 850 prophets of Baal and Asherah (1 Kings 18:21,40).

Eliphaz: one of Job's well-meaning but misguided comforters (Job 4:1).

Elizabeth: a righteous descendant of Aaron who was the wife of Zacharias and mother of John the Baptist (Luke 1:5,13).

Elisha: a prophet who served from approximately 850 to 800 BC in the northern kingdom (Israel) during the reigns of Jehoram, Jehu, Jehoahaz, and Joash. He not only prophesied and performed many miracles but also advised kings and helped the disadvantaged (2 Kings 2:14,19-21; 4:1-7; 5:1-14; 6:15-17).

Elkanah: the name of several biblical men. One was Hannah's husband and Samuel's father (1 Samuel 1:19).

Elohim (strong one): a Hebrew word translated *Lord* about 2570 times in the Old Testament as a name for God

(Nehemiah 2:4; Isaiah 54:5; Jeremiah 32:27). The name emphasizes God's might and sovereignty (Genesis 24:3; Isaiah 37:16; 54:5), His majesty and glory (Isaiah 40:28; 65:16), His role as the Savior (Genesis 17:8; 26:24; 28:13), His intimacy with His people (Genesis 48:15; Psalm 4:1; Jeremiah 23:23), and His role as Judge (Psalm 50:6; 58:11; 75:7).

Emmaus: a small village not far from Jerusalem. On the road from Jerusalem to Emmaus, the risen Christ appeared to two disciples and revealed that He was the fulfillment of multiple Old Testament Scriptures (Luke 24:13).

Endor: a city near Mount Tabor. King Saul consulted a medium who lived there (1 Samuel 28:7).

Enoch: the eldest son of Cain. He built a city east of Eden (Genesis 4:17).

Epaphroditus: a messenger from the church at Philippi who delivered a gift to the apostle Paul during Paul's Roman imprisonment (Philippians 2:25-30; 4:10-18).

Ephesians: a circular letter Paul wrote in AD 61 to several churches. Paul describes God's eternal and sovereign purpose for the church (Ephesians 1:6-14) as well as believers' spiritual blessing and endowment in Jesus Christ (2:4-10). Believers should therefore live a life worthy of the high calling with which they have been called (4:1). Paul also explains that all things in the universe find their ultimate unity in the person of Jesus Christ (4:1-16). This especially includes the church, where Jews and Gentiles—believers from every nation in the world—are united in Christ.

Ephesus: a leading commercial and trade center of the ancient world, characterized by luxurious homes, elegant buildings, and wide avenues. About 100 aristocrats owned most of the land around the city and controlled the local government. Ephesus was well known for its temple of the Roman goddess Diana (Greek: *Artemis*), one of the seven wonders of the world. During Paul's third missionary tour, he spent about three years in Ephesus building up the church (Acts 19).

Ephod: a sacred garment worn by the high priest. It was made of fine linen with colorful embroidery (Exodus 28:4-12,31).

Ephraim: the younger of Joseph's two sons, as well as his descendants, who became one of Israel's tribes, and the land they inherited (Genesis 41:52; 46:20). Also, a name for the northern kingdom (Israel—Isaiah 11:13).

Epicureans: the followers of Epicurus, who taught that there is no afterlife and promoted a life of pleasure (Acts 17:18).

Epistle (letter): one of the 21 New Testament letters. Each is inspired by the Holy Spirit (2 Timothy 3:16). Letters became a very important form of communication in the Greek-speaking world about 300 years prior to the time of Jesus. They typically included an introduction (the sender's name and some form of greeting), the body, and a conclusion. They were generally hand delivered by a messenger. Many of the New Testament epistles or letters were written to brand-new churches that had certain problems or questions (1 and 2 Thessalonians are examples).

Esau: Edom, Isaac and Rebekah's firstborn twin son who was characterized by being hairy (Genesis 25:25). He is famous for foolishly surrendering his birthright for a hearty serving of soup (Genesis 25:29-34). Also, his descendants and the land they inhabited (Genesis 36:16; Numbers 20:14-21).

Eschatology: from two Greek words—*eschatos* (last or last things) and *logos* (study of). Eschatology is the study of last things, or study of the end times, particularly as related to the second coming of Christ and the events preceding and following this great event. This word is not in the Bible.

Esther: the heroine of an anonymous Old Testament book written around 465 BC. Interestingly, the book never mentions God, but it shows Him constantly and providentially working behind the scenes. It describes an insidious plot by the evil Haman to destroy the Jews and God's deliverance.

To bring about this end, God providentially promoted Esther, a beautiful, faithful, and brave Jewish girl, to become the queen of the Persian king Xerxes I, who ruled Persia from 486 to 465 BC. Her cousin, Mordecai, helped her see that she had become queen "for such a time as this" (Esther 4:14).

Eternal Life: a gift available to those who believe in Christ as Savior (John 3:15-16; 5:24; 6:40,47; 12:25). It is both quantitative (continuing into eternity) and qualitative (including heavenly characteristics here and now).

Ethiopia: the geographical territory just south of Egypt on the Nile River in modern-day Sudan (Ezekiel 38:5).

Eunice: the mother of Timothy (2 Timothy 1:5; 3:15).

Eunuch: a castrated guard of the royal harem (Esther 2:3).

Euphrates River: the longest river of western Asia (almost 1800 miles). It begins in modern-day Turkey, flows toward the Mediterranean Sea, eventually converges with the Tigris River, and then flows into the Persian Gulf (Exodus 23:31; Deuteronomy 1:7).

Evangelism: the proclamation of the good news of salvation in Jesus Christ (John 3:16; Romans 5:8; 10:14-15; Ephesians 4:11; 2 Timothy 4:5; 2 Peter 3:9). This word is not in most Bibles.

Eve (giver of life): the first woman and Adam's wife (Genesis 3:20; 4:1), through whom the rest of humanity was born.

Exile: living in a foreign land to avoid persecution or as a result of judgment. The two most significant periods of exile for the Jews began with the fall of Israel to the Assyrians in 722 BC and the destruction of Judah by the Babylonians in 597–581 BC.

Exodus: a book written by Moses around 1440 BC about Israel's slavery in Egypt and their departure as a result of the ten plagues God inflicted on Pharaoh and the Egyptians at the hand of Moses (chapters 1–15). The book also deals with God's establishment of Israel's theocracy under Moses by means of the covenant He instituted at Sinai (chapters 16–40). In this covenant, God gave instructions for the ordering of life among the Hebrew people through the commandments given to Moses at Mount Sinai. Exodus also provides detailed information about the tabernacle and the ministry of the priests.

Ezekiel: a prophet to the Jews in exile. Ezekiel was about 30 years old, training to be a priest, when God called him into service as a prophet. He was taken to Babylon with the other Jewish exiles.

Also, the book he wrote between 593 and 570 BC. It explains that God's judgment falls as a result of human sin, but it also contains words of hope and comfort to the Jews in exile. Ezekiel graphically portrays God regathering His people from the ends of the earth to Jerusalem, where a new temple would be built (Ezekiel 40).

Ezra: a Jewish priest who led a group of exiles back to Jerusalem. Also, the book he wrote between 457 and 444 BC. Zerubbabel had led a group of Jews back to Jerusalem nearly six decades earlier in order to rebuild the temple (1:1–2:70). Now Ezra was leading another group in order to rebuild (or reform) the people's spiritual lives

(7:1–8:36) according to God's law (9:1–10:44). This return was allowed by the decree of King Cyrus of Persia.

═══════════════════════════════════ **F**

Faith: "the assurance of things hoped for, the conviction of things not seen" (Hebrews 11:1). It is the Word of God that strengthens the faith of believers. John's Gospel tells us that "these things [in John's Gospel] have been written so that you may believe" (John 20:31). Paul tells us that "faith comes from hearing the message, and the message is heard through the word of Christ" (Romans 10:17 NIV).

Faithfulness: consistent loyalty, trustworthiness, and assured reliance on God (Acts 16:1; 1 Corinthians 4:17; 2 Corinthians 6:15; Ephesians 1:1; Colossians 1:2; 1 Timothy 4:3,12).

Fall: a theological term (not included in the Bible) referring to the sin of the first man and woman, Adam and Eve, and the subsequent plunging of the human race into a state of sin and corruption. When Adam and Eve sinned, it did not just affect them in an isolated way. It affected the entire human race. Ever since then, every human being born into the world has been born in a state of sin (Psalm 51:5; Romans 5:12,19; 1 Corinthians 15:21-22).

False Apostles: deceitful individuals who masquerade

as apostles of Christ and teach destructive heresies (2 Corinthians 11:13). Christ commends those who stand against false apostles (Revelation 2:2).

False Christs: deceitful individuals who pose as God's Messiah, preach a counterfeit gospel, and offer a counterfeit salvation (Matthew 24:24; Mark 13:22; 2 Corinthians 11:4).

False Prophet: a lieutenant of the antichrist during the future tribulation period. He will promote false doctrine and entice people to worship the antichrist (Revelation 13:11-15).

False Prophets: teachers who pretend to be genuine spokesmen for God but in fact promote false doctrine (Matthew 7:15-16; Acts 20:28-30; 2 Corinthians 11:2-3).

Familiar Spirit: an alleged spirit from the realm of the dead that sorcerers, witches, or necromancers seek to summon (Leviticus 20:27; 2 Chronicles 33:6; Isaiah 29:4 KJV).

Fasting (cover the mouth): abstaining from food for spiritual reasons (Zechariah 7:3,5; 8:19; Matthew 6:16-18). In the Old Testament, only one fast was commanded, and that was on the annual Day of Atonement (Leviticus 16:29-31 NIV). Only after the fall of Jerusalem were additional fasts instituted (see Zechariah 7:3,5; 8:19).

Father: one's biological father (Genesis 2:24), an ancestor (Deuteronomy 1:11; 1 Kings 15:11), an elder (Judges 17:10;

18:19; 1 Samuel 10:12; 2 Kings 2:12), or God (Romans 1:7; 1 Corinthians 1:3; 2 Corinthians 1:2-3; Galatians 1:4).

Fatling: a young lamb to be slaughtered (2 Samuel 6:13; Isaiah 11:6; Ezekiel 39:18).

Fear of the Lord: believers' reverence for God that produces obedience in their lives (Deuteronomy 32:6; Isaiah 1:2; 63:16; 64:8 ; Hosea 11:1). The fear of the Lord is the beginning of knowledge (Proverbs 1:7; 9:10; 15:33).

Feast of Booths or **Feast of Tabernacles**: a commemoration of the Israelites' wilderness wandering. It included the building of temporary shelters (Leviticus 23:42-43).

Feast of Harvest or **Feast of Weeks** or **Pentecost**: a celebration held in the spring at the beginning of the wheat harvest to thank God for providing grain (Exodus 23:16; 34:22; Leviticus 23:15-21).

Feast of Unleavened Bread or **Passover**: a remembrance of God's deliverance of the Israelites from their bondage in Egypt (Ezekiel 45:21).

Felix: the Roman procurator of Judea during Paul's arraignment (Acts 24:25).

Firmament: the atmosphere and outer space (Genesis 1:7,14-17 KJV and NKJV).

First and the Last: a title of our eternal Almighty God (Isaiah 44:6; 48:12) that Christ ascribed to Himself (Revelation 1:17; 2:8; 22:13).

First Fruits: the initial harvest, which was offered to God (Exodus 23:16). Used figuratively of believers (James 1:18) and of Christ (1 Corinthians 15:2-3).

First Resurrection: the restoration of life to believers who have died (Luke 14:14; John 5:28-29; Revelation 20:4-6). This occurs after the tribulation and before the millennial kingdom, and it leads to eternal blessing. *See also* Second Resurrection.

Firstborn: the son who was the preeminent family heir regardless of whether he was literally born first (Genesis 25:23,31,34; 49:3; Deuteronomy 21:17; 1 Chronicles 5:1; Psalm 89:27; Hebrews 12:16). He received a double portion of the family inheritance. Used metaphorically of Christ (Colossians 1:15), who is preeminent and supreme over all creation.

Flesh: the physical body of a man or animal (Genesis 2:21; 41:2; Psalm 102:5), the human nature of Christ in the Incarnation (John 1:14), or metaphorically, man's unrenewed sinful nature (Romans 6:19; 7:5; 8:4-12).

Flood: specifically, the deluge that came upon humankind because the whole earth became filled with violence and corruption (Genesis 6:14–9:18). The flood was apparently worldwide and universal, for the waters climbed so high on the earth that "all the high mountains under the entire heavens were covered" (Genesis 7:19 NIV). They rose so greatly on the earth that they "covered the mountains to a depth of more than twenty feet" (verse 20 NIV). The flood lasted some 377 days (nearly 54 weeks), indicating more than just local flooding. The Bible also says that every living thing that moved on the earth perished: "Everything on dry land that had the breath of life in its nostrils died. Every living thing on the face of the earth was wiped out…Only Noah was left, and those with him in the ark" (verses 22-23 NIV).

Fold: an animal pen (Isaiah 13:20 KJV). Figuratively, Israel (Jeremiah 25:30) or the church (John 10:1,16).

Footstool: a foot support positioned in front of a throne (2 Chronicles 9:18). Earth is God's footstool (Psalm 110:1; Isaiah 66:1; Matthew 5:35). Christ's enemies will be made His footstool—a figure of speech describing Christ's power and authority (Psalm 110:1; Luke 20:43).

Foreigner: Gentile (Exodus 22:21; 23:9; Leviticus 19:33-34).

Foreknowledge: God's complete knowledge of all that will transpire in the future (Acts 2:23; Romans 8:29; 11:2; 1 Peter 1:2). Only God in His omniscience knows the future. In Isaiah 46:9-11 ESV, God Himself makes this affirmation: "I am God, and there is no other; I am God, and there is none like me, declaring the end from the beginning and from ancient times things not yet done, saying, My counsel shall stand, and I will accomplish all my purpose…I have spoken, and I will bring it to pass; I have purposed, and I will do it."

Forerunner: figuratively used of John the Baptist, who prepared the way for Jesus (Luke 1:17), and of Jesus, who prepared a way for us (Hebrews 6:20).

Forgiveness: a pardoning or excusing of sins, faults, and shortcomings (Acts 16:31). God affirms, "Their sins and lawless acts I will remember no more" (Hebrews 10:17 NIV). Scripture promises, "as far as the east is from the west, so far has He removed our transgressions from us" (Psalm 103:12).

Fornication: illicit sexual intercourse. Christians are commanded to abstain from fornication (Acts 15:20). The apostle Paul strongly affirmed that the body is not for fornication and that a man should flee it (1 Corinthians 6:13,18). Christians must not forget that the body is the temple of the Holy Spirit (1 Corinthians 6:19). The Ephesians were instructed that fornication should not be even once named or spoken of among them (5:3).

Frankincense: a fragrant tree resin used to make perfume (Exodus 30:34; Isaiah 60:6; Jeremiah 6:20). It was used in the tabernacle and temple (Exodus 30:34; Leviticus 2:1-2) and offered as an expensive gift (Isaiah 60:6; Matthew 2:11).

Freewill Offering: a spontaneous, voluntary sacrifice (Exodus 35:29; Leviticus 22:23; Ezra 3:5).

=== **G**

Gabriel (mighty one of God): a powerful angel who stands in God's presence, evidently in some preeminent sense (Luke 1:19). He flies very swiftly when carrying out God's bidding (Daniel 9:21 KJV, NKJV) and brings major revelations to God's people (Daniel 8:16; 9:21).

Gad: Jacob's seventh son (his first with Zilpah, Leah's servant—Genesis 30:11; 46:16-18). Also, Gad's descendants, who became one of Israel's tribes, and the land they inherited (Numbers 32:1-5). Also the name of a prophet during the time of David (2 Samuel 24:11-19; 1 Chronicles 21:9-19).

Gaius: the name of several biblical persons, including several ministry associates of the apostle Paul (Acts 20:4; Romans 16:23; 1 Corinthians 1:14) and a Christian in Asia Minor to whom John addressed his third epistle (3 John 1:1).

Galatians: a book the apostle Paul wrote to a church in the Roman province of Galatia in AD 50. Paul confirmed his authority as a genuine apostle of Jesus Christ (Galatians 1:10–2:21). Apparently Judaizers had infiltrated some of Paul's congregations and challenged his credentials. They were unhappy with the way Paul freely invited Gentiles to come to God. They argued that in order to make the gospel more appealing to Gentiles, Paul removed certain legal requirements (including circumcision). Their purpose was therefore to "Judaize" these Gentile believers—that is, persuade them that, after believing in Christ, they must take an additional step and become Jews through circumcision, eat only ceremonially clean foods, and participate in certain Jewish feast days (Acts 15:24; 20:29-30). Paul refuted such ideas in this book.

Galilee: the land west of the Sea of Galilee (Matthew 2:22; Acts 10:37). The Gospels of Matthew, Mark, and Luke focus on Christ's ministry in Galilee. Jesus gave 19 of His 32 parables in Galilee. *See also* Sea of Galilee.

Gallio: a Greek government official under the emperor Claudius. Gallio was in office when Paul visited Corinth (Acts 18:12-16).

Gamaliel: the name of several biblical people, including a chief of the tribe of Manasseh (Numbers 1:10; 2:20; 7:54,59), and a Pharisee and member of the Sanhedrin who instructed Paul (Acts 22:3).

Garasenes: inhabitants of Gadara, where Jesus cast many demons out of a man and into a herd of swine (Mark 5:1; Luke 8:26,37).

Gath: a prominent Philistine city that was the birthplace of Goliath (1 Samuel 17:4).

Gaza: a prominent Philistine city on the Mediterranean shore (Deuteronomy 2:23; 1 Kings 4:24; Jeremiah 25:20).

Gehenna: a metaphor for hell (2 Kings 23:10; Matthew 10:28). It refers to a valley where garbage and the bodies of dead animals were dumped and continually burned.

Genesis: the first book of Moses, written between 1445 and 1405 BC, which describes the beginnings of the universe, including humanity (Genesis 1–2), the fall of man and the consequences of that fall (3), the lives of Adam and his family (4–5), Noah and the worldwide flood (6–10), the judgment that took place at the Tower of Babel, after which the nations were dispersed (11), the lives of the patriarchs Abraham, Isaac, Esau, and Jacob (12–36), Joseph's betrayal by his brothers and their reconciliation (37–45), and Jacob's move to Egypt with his family (46–50).

Gennesaret: a town of Naphtali, also called Chinnereth (Joshua 19:35). The Sea of Galilee is also called the Lake of Gennesaret (Luke 5:1).

Gentiles: people who are not Jews (Matthew 4:15; Romans 3:29; 11:11,13; 15:10; 16:4; Galatians 2:8,12,14; Ephesians 3:1). Sometimes used scornfully.

Gethsemane: the garden where Jesus prayed prior to His arrest (Matthew 26:36; Mark 14:32).

Ghost: spirit (Matthew 14:26). Also, a person's life (Job 11:20; Jeremiah 15:9; Matthew 27:50 KJV) and the Holy Spirit (Matthew 1:18 KJV).

Giant: ancestors of some Philistine warriors (1 Chronicles 20:4). Also, the Nephilim in Genesis 6:4 (NKJV).

Gideon: a judge in Israel who defeated the Midianites (Judges 6–8; 1 Samuel 12:11; Isaiah 9:4; 10:26; Hebrews 11:32).

Gifts of the Holy Spirit: special abilities bestowed sovereignly by God on individual believers for the purpose of edifying the church, the body of Christ. These gifts include teaching, pastoring, evangelizing, the message of wisdom, the message of knowledge, faith, healing, miraculous powers, prophecy, distinguishing between spirits, speaking in different tongues, and the interpretation of tongues (Romans 12:3-8; 1 Corinthians 12:8-10; Ephesians 4:7-13).

Gilead: the region east of Jordan (Genesis 31:21). Also, the name of several biblical persons (Numbers 36:1; Judges 11:1; 1 Chronicles 5:14).

Gilgal: the place of the Israelites' first encampment in the Promised Land (Joshua 9:6; 10:6).

Gleaning: gathering food from the unreaped corners of farmers' fields. Poor families in Israel were allowed to do this so they would not starve (Leviticus 19:9-10; 23:22; Deuteronomy 24:21).

Glorify: to honor and worship God (John 12:28; 13:31-32; 17:4-5).

Glory: the luminous manifestation of God. Brilliant light consistently accompanied the manifestation of His glory (Matthew 17:2-3; 1 Timothy 6:16; Revelation 1:16).

Gnash: to grind, as in grinding the teeth (Job 16:9; Psalm 112:10; Lamentations 2:16), denoting strong emotions, such as rage or sorrow.

God: the personal Spirit who is the Creator and Sustainer of the universe and who is holy (Isaiah 6:3), eternal (1 Timothy 1:17), omnipotent (Isaiah 14:27), omniscient (Psalm 33:13-15; 139:11-12; 147:5), omnipresent (Psalm 139:7-8; Jeremiah 23:23-24), loving (1 John 4:8), and just (Zephaniah 3:5; Romans 3:26). He is both transcendent and immanent (Deuteronomy 4:39; Isaiah 57:15; Jeremiah 23:23-24) and is triune (Matthew 28:19; 2 Corinthians 13:14). His names include *Yahweh* ("Lord," Exodus 3:14-15), *Elohim* ("mighty God," Genesis 1:1), and *Adonai* ("Lord" or "Master," Genesis 18:27).

Godliness: holiness or piety (1 Timothy 4:8; 2 Peter 1:6).

Gog: the powerful leader of the end-times northern military coalition that will invade Israel (Ezekiel 38:2).

Golan: a city of refuge 12 miles northeast of the Sea of Galilee (Joshua 20:8).

Golden Calf: an idolatrous molten image of a calf that Aaron formed at Sinai and Moses destroyed (Exodus 32:1-10,19-24; Deuteronomy 9:16; Nehemiah 9:18).

Golgotha (place of a skull): the skull-shaped knoll where Jesus Christ was crucified (Matthew 27:33; Mark 15:22; John 19:17).

Goliath: a giant warrior among the Philistines who defied the armies of Israel for 40 days. David defeated him in a one-on-one confrontation (1 Samuel 17:4,51).

Gomer: one of the nations of the northern military coalition that will invade Israel in the end times (Ezekiel 38:1-6), probably modern-day Turkey or Germany.

Gomorrah: a wicked city near the Dead Sea destroyed by fire and brimstone as a judgment from God (Genesis 10:19; 13:10; 19:24,28).

Goshen: a territory northeast of the Nile delta where the Israelites lived and thrived when Joseph was in power in Egypt (Genesis 45:10; 46:28-31).

Gospel: the good news of salvation in Jesus Christ. The best single definition of the gospel is found in 1 Corinthians 15:3-4 (NIV): "For what I received I passed on to you as of first importance: that Christ died for our sins according to the Scriptures, that he was buried, that he was raised on the third day according to the Scriptures." The gospel, according to this passage, has four components: man is a sinner, Christ is the Savior, Christ died as man's substitute, and Christ rose from the dead.

Also, one of the first four books of the New Testament, which communicate Jesus' identity, His message, and His death and resurrection (Luke 1:1-4; John 20:30; 21:25). They are selective (Luke 1:1-4; John 20:30; 21:25) and focus primarily on His three-year ministry, with the exception of a short discussion of His birth and infancy (Matthew 1–2; Luke 1–2). God the Holy Spirit inspired these Gospels (2 Timothy 3:16; 2 Peter 1:21), so we can be assured that everything God wanted us to know about Jesus' life and ministry is there.

Grace (unmerited favor): *Unmerited* means this favor cannot be earned. Regarding salvation, the apostle Paul explains that God gives His incredible grace to those who actually deserve the opposite—that is, condemnation (Romans 5:1-11; Ephesians 2:8-9).

Graven Image: a sculptured idol designed as a object of worship (Deuteronomy 27:15 KJV; Psalm 97:7).

Great White Throne: the seat where Christ will judge unbelievers after the millennial kingdom and before casting them into the lake of fire (Revelation 20:11-15).

Greek: Gentile as opposed to Jew (Romans 2:9-10). Also, the language of the New Testament (Koine Greek).

Guilt: responsibility for a wrongdoing (Psalm 51). Also, a sense of remorseful awareness of having done something wrong (Genesis 3:8; Matthew 27:3).

Guilt Offering: a means of making restitution after breaking social, religious, or ritual obligations (Leviticus 5:15).

H

Habakkuk: an Old Testament prophet and contemporary of Jeremiah (seventh century BC). Also, the book he wrote, which wrestles with reasons why good and innocent people suffer while evil people so often seem to prosper. Specifically, Habakkuk asked why God allowed Babylonian pagans to defeat the people of God (Habakkuk 1:1-11). God answered that the Babylonians and all like them would eventually be destroyed, but those who trust in God will remain and be blessed (1:12–2:20). We must live by faith in God (2:4).

Hades: the New Testament counterpart to the Old Testament term *Sheol* (Luke 16:19-31). Hades is a temporary abode of the unbelieving dead. They will eventually be raised from the dead, judged at the Great White Throne judgment, and cast into the lake of fire (hell), which will be their permanent place of suffering throughout all eternity (Revelation 20:14-15).

Hagar: Sarah's handmaiden, whom she gave to her husband, Abraham, to bear children on her behalf (Genesis 16:1-2; 21:9-10).

Haggai: an Old Testament prophet and the book he wrote in approximately 520 BC. Haggai urged the Jews who had returned from exile to renew their commitment to God, to set their priorities straight, and to rebuild the temple (Haggai 1:1-11). Only then would they receive God's blessing.

Haggai sought to help them overcome a defeated state of mind and move on to obedience and service to God.

Hallelujah or **Alleluia** (praise Yahweh): an exclamation of praise (Psalm 106, 111–113, 135, 146–150; Revelation 19:1-6).

Ham: a son of Noah (Genesis 5:32).

Hannah: a wife of Elkanah and the mother of the prophet Samuel (1 Samuel 1:5; 2:21).

Hanukkah: a Jewish holy day commemorating the cleansing and rededication of the temple by Judas Maccabaeus in 164 BC (Ezra 6:16; John 10:22). This word is not in the Bible.

Heaven: the splendorous eternal abode of the righteous (1 Corinthians 2:9), where God Himself dwells (Revelation 21). It is also known as the heavenly country (Hebrews 11:13-16 NKJV), the paradise of God (Revelation 2:7), the holy city (Revelation 21:1-2), the home of righteousness (2 Peter 3:13), and the kingdom of light (Colossians 1:12).

Heavens: Scripture mentions three heavens: the earth's atmosphere (Job 35:5), the stellar universe (Genesis 1:17; Deuteronomy 17:3), and God's eternal dwelling place (2 Corinthians 12:2).

Hebrew: a descendant of Abraham, Isaac, and Jacob (Genesis 14:13; Exodus 1:15; 9:13). Also, the language of the Israelites and the Old Testament.

Hebrews: a New Testament book written to Jewish Christians (Hebrews 13:22) in approximately 68 AD. This "word of exhortation" draws heavily on the Old Testament and urges readers to remain steadfast in their commitment to Christ and His cause despite their heavy persecution by the Jewish high priest (10:32-34). The author of Hebrews calls his readers to move on to maturity in the Christian faith despite their trials (6:1).

Hebron: an ancient city midway between Jerusalem and Beersheba. Abraham buried Sarah there (Genesis 23:2), and David used it as a royal residence (2 Samuel 2:1).

Heifer: a young cow (Deuteronomy 21:4,6; Jeremiah 46:20).

Hell: the eternal abode of the unsaved, a place of unimaginable suffering also known as the lake of fire (Revelation 20:15), eternal fire (Matthew 25:41), a fiery furnace (Matthew 13:42 NIV), eternal punishment (Matthew 25:46), and destruction (2 Thessalonians 1:8-9). Of course, the greatest pain suffered by those in hell is exclusion from the presence of God. His presence brings fullness of joy (Psalm 16:11), so exclusion from His presence brings utter dismay.

Heresy (chosen opinion): an idea that denies a Scriptural doctrine (2 Peter 2:1).

Hermon: a sacred mountain on the northern boundary of Palestine (Deuteronomy 3:8; 4:48; Joshua 11:3,17; 12:1; 13:11).

Herod Agrippa I: the grandson of Herod the Great. He persecuted the church (Acts 12:1-23).

Herod Agrippa II: the son of Agrippa I and great-grandson of Herod the Great. He was the tetrarch of Tiberias, Abila, and Traconitis when the apostle Paul was on trial (Acts 25:13,23-27).

Herod Antipas: a son of Herod the Great. He was the tetrarch of Galilee and Perea who imprisoned and murdered John the Baptist (Matthew 14:1; Luke 3:1).

Herod Archelaus: a son of Herod the Great. He was the governor of Ituraea and Traconitis when Joseph, Mary, and Jesus moved from Egypt to Nazareth (Matthew 2:19-23).

Herod the Great: the stern and cruel king of Judea, Samaria, Ituraea, and Traconitis who ruled during the time of Jesus' birth and slaughtered the babies of Bethlehem (Matthew 2).

Herodians: Jewish political sympathizers of Herod's line of rulers (Matthew 22:16; Mark 3:6; 12:13; Luke 20:20).

Herodias: the wife of Herod Antipas (Matthew 14:3-11; Mark 6:17-28; Luke 3:19).

Hezekiah: a well-respected king of Judah who ruled for 29 years and stood against idolatry (2 Kings 18:20; 2 Chronicles 29–32; Isaiah 36–39).

High Place: a place for worship or sacrifice (1 Kings 13:32; 2 Kings 17:29).

High Priest: the chief among Jewish priests. Aaron was the first to hold this office (Exodus 29:7; Leviticus 8:12). On the annual Day of Atonement, the high priest sprinkled the blood of a sacrificial animal on the mercy seat of the ark of the covenant to symbolize the nation's repentance for the sins committed the previous year.

Hiram: the King of Tyre who helped David build his palace and helped Solomon build the temple (2 Samuel 5:11; 1 Kings 5:1; 9:11; 1 Chronicles 14:1; 2 Chronicles 2:3).

Hittites: a powerful people who lived near Hebron during the time of Abraham (Genesis 23:10-20).

Holiness: derives from a Greek word meaning "set apart" or "separated" and refers to being set apart from sin and all that is unclean (1 Thessalonians 3:13; 1 Peter 1:15).

Holy of Holies or **Most Holy Place**: the innermost portion of the tabernacle and temple, where no one was permitted to enter except the high priest, and then only once a year on the Day of Atonement to offer a sacrifice for the sins of the people (Exodus 25:10-16). The ark of the covenant symbolized God's presence (1 Samuel 4:3-22) and was kept in the holy of holies.

Holy Place: a portion of the tabernacle or temple just outside the holy of holies that contained important furnishings for Hebrew worship. The altar of incense stood in front of the veil to the holy of holies (Exodus 30:1-10). The table of showbread held 12 loaves of bread presented by the 12 tribes of Israel each Sabbath as a meal offering (Exodus 25:23-29). The bread was not for God to eat, but was a symbol of spiritual food (Leviticus 24:5-9). The golden lampstand was set on the south wall of the holy place (Exodus 26:35), opposite the table of showbread on the north, so that the light would be reflected toward the table. The light was to burn perpetually and be serviced each evening and morning (Exodus 27:21; Leviticus 24:1-4).

Holy Spirit: the third person of the Trinity (Matthew 28:19; 2 Corinthians 13:14). The Holy Spirit is God, for Scripture reveals that the Holy Spirit has the attributes of deity, including omnipresence (Psalm 139:7), omniscience (1 Corinthians 2:10), omnipotence (Romans 15:19), holiness (John 16:7-14), and eternality (Hebrews 9:14). We know He is a person, for He has mind (Romans 8:27; 1 Corinthians 2:10), emotions (Ephesians 4:30), and will (1 Corinthians 12:11). The Holy Spirit inspired Scripture (2 Timothy 3:16; 2 Peter 1:21), He was instrumental in the Incarnation of Christ (Luke 1:35), and He gives spiritual gifts to Christians (1 Corinthians 12:11).

Homosexual: a person who is attracted sexually to members of his or her own sex. Homosexuality is considered a vile sin against God (Leviticus 18:22; Romans 1:26; 1 Corinthians 6:9).

Hophni: one of the two sons of Eli (1 Samuel 1:3; 2:34), who, because of their scandalous conduct, brought God's curse on their family (1 Samuel 2:22,12-36; 3:11-14).

Horeb: another name for Mount Sinai, where God appeared to Moses and gave him the Ten Commandments (Exodus 3:1; 17:6; 33:6; Psalm 106:19).

Hosanna (save [us]): an acclamation of praise and adoration (Psalm 118:25 NIV; Matthew 21:9).

Hosea: an Old Testament prophet and the book he wrote in approximately 710 BC, which depicts the heartfelt pain he suffered because of the unfaithfulness of his wife, Gomer. This gave him insight to God's response when His own people are unfaithful to Him. Just as Gomer had been unfaithful to the marriage covenant, so the Israelites had been unfaithful to the covenant God made with them (Hosea 2:2-5; 6:4-11; 8:1-14). They committed spiritual adultery and turned away from God, just as Gomer had committed physical adultery. In their unfaithfulness, the Israelites engaged in an adulterous relationship with Canaanite deities (such as Baal). Yet just as Hosea loved Gomer, God still loved the Israelites despite their unfaithfulness (11:1-12).

Host of Heaven: the starry universe (Genesis 2:1). Also, God's army of angels (1 Kings 22:19).

Hyssop: a plant often used during purification rituals (Psalm 51:7).

Iconium: a capital city in Asia Minor that Paul and Barnabas visited during Paul's first missionary tour (Acts 13:50-51).

Idolatry: the worship of false gods or idols (Exodus 20:4; Leviticus 26:1; 2 Kings 9:22). Many pagan nations believed the different gods were behind various aspects of the world of nature. For example, they might have worshipped a god of crops, another god of light related to the sun or the moon, and other gods related to the stars. Still other gods might be related to health and healing or to protection of the animals of the land. Many ancient idolaters believed that in order to be successful in life, they had to please the gods so they wouldn't treat them cruelly. Israel was warned to steer clear of such idolatry (Exodus 20:4).

Immanuel (God with us): a messianic term referring to Jesus Christ (Isaiah 7:14; Matthew 1:23).

Impute (put to an account): to give someone responsibility, blame, or credit for something (Romans 5:13). Believers enjoy a great exchange—Christ bears the penalty for our sins, and we receive the benefits of His righteousness (Romans 3:24-30; 2 Corinthians 5:21).

Incarnation: the miracle in which Jesus, the eternal Son of God, took on a human nature while fully retaining His divine nature. This word is not in the Bible, but innumerable passages in the New Testament confirm Christ's full humanity in the Incarnation. Hebrews 2:14 (NIV) tells us, for example, that since God's children "have flesh and blood, he too shared in their humanity so that by his death he might destroy him who holds the power of death—that is, the devil" (*see also* Romans 8:3; Galatians 4:4-5; 1 Timothy 3:16). And yet He fully retained His divine nature (Philippians 2:5-11; Colossians 2:9), so that in the Incarnation Jesus was the God-man.

Inspiration (of Scripture): God's superintendence of the human authors of the Bible so that, using their own individual personalities and even their writing styles, they composed and recorded without error His revelation to humankind in the words of the original autographs (2 Timothy 3:16).

Intermediate State: This phrase is not in the Bible, but it refers to the biblical description of our existence between the time our mortal bodies die and the time we receive resurrection bodies in the future (Revelation 6:9-11).

Isaac (laughter): the son of promise born to Abraham and Sarah in their old age (Genesis 17:17; 21:5; Galatians 4:22-23). His name points to the joy derived from his birth. When Abraham and Sarah heard they would have a son in their old age, they laughed (Genesis 17:17-19; 18:9-15). Isaac carried on the covenant first given to his father,

Abraham. The New Testament calls him a child of promise (Galatians 4:22-23), and he was a man of good character. He trusted in God (Genesis 22:6,9), practiced regular prayer (Genesis 26:25; Hebrews 11:11-17), and sought peace (Genesis 26:20-22).

Isaiah (the Lord saves): the greatest of the Old Testament prophets and the book he wrote between 740 and 680 BC. The book is the third longest in the Bible and contains more prophetic references to Jesus than any other book in the Old Testament. Isaiah predicted the Messiah's virgin birth (7:14), His deity and kingdom (9:1-7), His righteous reign (11:2-5), His vicarious suffering and death (52:13–53:12), and much more. No wonder the great composer Handel based so much of his musical masterpiece *The Messiah* on the book of Isaiah. Isaiah's name fits his ministry because salvation was an important part of his message to the people of Judah.

Iscariot: a reference to Judas, Christ's disciple and betrayer (Mark 3:19; John 12:4; 13:26).

Ishmael: a son born to Abraham and Hagar, Sarah's handmaiden (Genesis 16:15; 17:23).

Israel: a name conferred on the patriarch Jacob at Peniel (Genesis 32:28). Also, the 12 tribes that descended from his 12 sons and the land they inherited (Joshua 3:17; 7:25; Judges 8:27; Jeremiah 3:21).

J

Jabez: a descendant of Judah. "God granted him that which he requested" in his famous prayer (1 Chronicles 4:9-10 KJV).

Jacob (he supplants): a son of Isaac. He was a supplanter, for he took hold of his brother Esau's birthright (Genesis 25:29-34), his father's blessing and inheritance (27:1-29), and his father-in-law's flocks (30:25-43).

Jairus: a ruler of the synagogue at Capernaum whose daughter Jesus restored to life (Mark 5:22; Luke 8:41).

Jambres: an Egyptian who opposed Moses (2 Timothy 3:8).

James: Jesus' oldest half-brother and the leader of the Jerusalem church (Acts 12:17). Also, the book he wrote between AD 44 and 49, which emphasizes righteous conduct and the need to be a doer of God's word and not just a hearer (James 1:22-25). James stresses that faith without works is dead (2:14-26). Our faith in Christ must show itself in the way we live—in all areas of life, including not showing partiality, controlling the tongue, having a right attitude toward money, and being humble, patient, and prayerful (2–5). Those who claim to have faith but do not show that faith in the way they live have a spurious faith.

Jannes: an Egyptian who opposed Moses (2 Timothy 3:8).

Japheth: a son of Noah (Genesis 5:32; 6:10; 7:13).

Jasper: a glittering precious stone of various colors that was included in the high priest's breastplate (Exodus 28:20).

Jephthah: the ninth judge of Israel. He delivered Israel from the oppression of the Ammonites (Judges 11:1-33).

Jeremiah: an Old Testament prophet. Also, the book he wrote between 627 and 570 BC. Jeremiah was given a harsh message to deliver to the people, and he felt inadequate in fulfilling the prophetic task to which he was called (Jeremiah 1:6-10). For decades he warned the Israelites of an impending judgment, but he was virtually ignored (2–35). The people remained in such horrible sins as flagrant idol worship, adultery, injustice, tyranny against the helpless, dishonesty, and more. Because of such sins, the people were rushing toward judgment. And because Jeremiah pointed toward a coming judgment, his life was often threatened by political and religious leaders (36–38). The judgment that finally came upon the people of God was the Babylonian exile (Jeremiah 39–45).

Jericho: a city in Canaan northeast of Jerusalem whose outer walls miraculously fell during Joshua's siege (Joshua 3:16; 6:1; 1 Kings 16:34).

Jeroboam: the name of the first and fourteenth kings of Israel (Jeroboam I and Jeroboam II). The first was the son of Nebat, an Ephraimite, by a woman named Zeruah

(1 Kings 11:26). The second was the son and successor of Jehoash (2 Kings 14:23).

Jerusalem: the capital city of Judah and the scene of Jesus' arrest, trial, crucifixion, and resurrection. The city itself rests in the Judean hills at about 2640 feet above sea level. During the time of Jesus, its population was probably about a quarter of a million. In Jewish thinking in biblical times, no city could possibly compare with Jerusalem. Israelites from all around traveled to Jerusalem for the three major festivals and to pay the annual temple tax. Jerusalem was the geographical heart of the Jewish religion. Jesus Himself made a number of visits to Jerusalem (Luke 2:22-51; 13:34).

King David captured the city in the tenth century BC. His son Solomon made Jerusalem the center of religious life and built a magnificent temple there. Jerusalem and the temple built by Herod were utterly destroyed in AD 70 by Rome, fulfilling Jesus' prediction (Matthew 24:2).

Jesse: the grandson of Boaz and Ruth. He was David's father (Ruth 4:17, 22; Matthew 1:5-6; Luke 3:32).

Jesus Christ (the Lord is salvation): the eternal Son of God, born as a human through the virgin Mary (Luke 1:31). There are numerous evidences for His absolute deity. For example, He is called God (Hebrews 1:8), Lord (Matthew 22:43-44), and King of kings and Lord of lords (Revelation 19:16). He also has all the attributes of deity, including omnipotence (Matthew 28:18), omniscience

(John 1:48), omnipresence (Matthew 18:20), and immutability (Hebrews 13:8).

A comparison of the Old and New Testaments provides powerful testimony to Jesus' identity as Yahweh. For example, in Zechariah 12:10 (NIV), Yahweh says, "They will look on me, the one they have pierced." Though Yahweh is speaking, this is obviously a reference to Christ's future crucifixion (Revelation 1:7). Certainly Jesus was worshipped as God many times according to the Gospel accounts. He accepted worship from Thomas (John 20:28), the angels (Hebrews 1:6), some wise men (Matthew 2:11), a leper (Matthew 8:2), and many others.

The miracles of Jesus provide further evidence about His divine identity. Jesus' miracles are often called *signs* in the New Testament, for signs always signify something—in this case, that Jesus is the divine Messiah. Some of Jesus' more notable miracles include turning water into wine (John 2:7-8), walking on the sea (Matthew 14:25; Mark 6:48; John 6:19), calming a stormy sea (Matthew 8:26; Mark 4:39; Luke 8:24), feeding 5000 men and their families (Matthew 14:19; Mark 6:41; Luke 9:16; John 6:11), raising Lazarus from the dead (John 11:43-44), and causing the disciples to catch a great number of fish (Luke 5:5-6).

Jesus' teachings were always presented as being ultimate and final. He never wavered in this. He unflinchingly placed His teachings above those of Moses and the prophets—and in a Jewish culture at that! He always spoke in His own authority. He never said, "Thus saith the Lord…" as did the prophets; He always said, "Truly I say to you…" He never retracted anything He said, never guessed or spoke with uncertainty, never made revisions, never contradicted Himself, and never apologized for what He said. He even asserted that "heaven and earth will pass away, but My words will not pass away" (Mark 13:31), elevating His words directly to the realm of heaven. How awesome is Jesus!

Jethro: the father-in-law of Moses and a priest in Midian (Exodus 3:1; 4:18; 18:1-12).

Jew: a descendant of Judah, son of Jacob (2 Kings 16:6). Sometime following the Babylonian captivity, the word came to refer to all descendants of Abraham, Isaac, and Jacob who lived in the hill country of Judah (2 Chronicles 32:18; Jeremiah 32:12; 34:9; 38:19). In New Testament times, the term likewise referred to Israelites in general (as opposed to Gentiles—Galatians 2:14; Titus 1:14).

Jezebel: the pagan and cruel wife of Ahab who heavily promoted Baal worship (1 Kings 16:31).

Jezreel: a city of Issachar (Joshua 19:18) where the kings of Israel often resided (1 Kings 18:45; 21:1; 2 Kings 9:30).

Joab: the name of several biblical persons, including a general in King David's army who enjoyed a successful military career (2 Samuel 2:13; 10:7; 11:1; 1 Kings 11:15).

Job: a book written by an unknown author prior to 1445

BC. It deals with a common problem: If God is good and just, why do good people suffer? (Job 1:13-22). Job was an upright man who had done nothing wrong, and yet catastrophe overwhelmed him at every side. He lost his possessions as well as his family, and he was engulfed in heinous physical suffering (Job 1:13-22). In the end, God restored Job's health and his possessions, and all was well. His faith in God, even in the midst of suffering, is the key lesson of the book.

Joel: an Old Testament prophet (the son of Pethuel) and the book he wrote in about 835 BC. Joel focused on the day of judgment that was coming upon God's people for their sins (Joel 1:15–2:11), which would be far worse than a plague of locusts. He called the people to repentance (2:12-17), explaining that God cannot ignore sin and that blessing follows obedience.

John: one of Jesus' three closest disciples. Also, the Gospel he wrote in approximately AD 90 to persuade men to trust in Christ, the divine Messiah and the Savior and Redeemer of the world (John 20:31).

John 1, 2, and 3: letters written by the aging apostle John in approximately AD 90 to correct an early strain of Gnosticism. Apparently some Gnostic teachers were conducting an itinerant ministry in John's congregations and making some converts. John wrote his epistles to warn true followers of Jesus Christ against such heresies. Of great concern to John were the Gnostic errors about Jesus. The primary issue was Jesus' identity: Was He both human and divine? The Gnostics tried to argue that a spiritual Christ did not actually become human but rather entered into the human Jesus at the time of the baptism and left the human Jesus before the crucifixion. Here's John's response: "This is how you can recognize the Spirit of God: Every spirit that acknowledges that Jesus Christ has come in the flesh is from God, but every spirit that does not acknowledge Jesus is not from God. This is the spirit of the antichrist, which you have heard is coming and even now is already in the world" (1 John 4:2-3 NIV).

John the Baptist: the cousin of Jesus who was miraculously born to Zacharias and Elizabeth in their old age (Luke 1:5-30). He was an unusual character—he lived in the desert, his clothing consisted of camel's hair (not too comfortable), and he ate locusts and wild honey for breakfast, lunch, and dinner. He prepared the way for the coming of the divine Messiah (Isaiah 40:3; John 1:15,23,30). Jesus said there was no human being greater than John the Baptist (Matthew 11:11).

Jonah: the son of Amittai who was an Old Testament prophet of the northern kingdom. Also, the book he wrote in about 760 BC during the reign of Jeroboam II. God commanded him to witness to the inhabitants of Nineveh, the capital of Assyria (a pagan nation). Jonah was initially resistant and tried to escape. God providentially brought Jonah back by having him swallowed by a big fish, which vomited him up on the beach where he was supposed to be (Jonah 1:17). Giving heed to God's providential actions, Jonah did as he was told and communicated the divine message to the Ninevites. They listened to Jonah's message and promptly repented, thereby averting a terrible judgment (3:6-10). This upset Jonah, for he did not want God to bless these pagans (4:1-3).

Jonathan: the name of several biblical persons. The most significant was the eldest son of King Saul and a very close friend of David (1 Samuel 13:2; 2 Samuel 1:22-23; 1 Chronicles 12:2).

Joppa: an ancient city on the Mediterranean 30 miles northwest of Jerusalem (2 Chronicles 2:16; Ezra 3:7). This is where Jonah embarked for Tarshish (Jonah 1:3).

Jordan: the chief (and longest) river of Palestine, flowing north to south down a deep valley in the heart of the country (Genesis 32:10; Joshua 3:17; Judges 8:4).

Joseph: Jacob's eleventh son (his first with Rachel). God providentially elevated him to a position of great authority in Egypt (Genesis 37:34-35; 39:1-6,20; 41:37-57) and used him to save Egypt (as well as his own family—the seed of the nation of Israel) from famine.

Joshua: Moses' protégé, who led Israel into the Promised Land. Also, the book he wrote between 1405 and 1385 BC. The book focuses on Israel's entry into Canaan (Joshua 1:1–5:15), conquest (6:1–12:24), and division of the land among the 12 tribes of Israel (13:1–24:33), all under the effective leadership of Joshua. This was all a fulfillment of the land promises given to Abraham and his descendants (Genesis 15:7; 26:2).

Josiah: the son of Amon who succeeded him on the throne of Judah (2 Kings 22:1; 2 Chronicles 34:1).

Jubilee: also called the year of liberty (Ezekiel 46:17), this was to be a year of emancipation in which the ancient Hebrews freed their slaves, forgave debts, and returned properties to their original owners (Leviticus 13–34; 25:39-54; 27:16-24). Scripture does not record Israel ever obeying the command to celebrate the year of jubilee.

Judah: Jacob and Leah's fourth son. Also, Judah's descendants, who became one of Israel's tribes, and the land they inherited. This tribe formed the nucleus of the southern kingdom, which was also known as Judah (Genesis 29:35; 37:26; 44:14; 49:8-10; Numbers 1:27; Judges 1:8; 2 Samuel 2:4).

Judaism: the religion of the Jews (Galatians 1:13-14). Jews believe that the entirety of God's Word is communicated in the Old Testament, and they give special attention to the Torah, God's Law, found in the first five books of the Old Testament. Their primary confession of faith is the Shema, which affirms that Yahweh is the one true God (Deuteronomy 6:4).

Judas: the name of several New Testament personalities,

the most famous being Iscariot, who betrayed Jesus Christ (Matthew 10:4; Luke 22:3; John 13:27; 18:2).

Jude: a younger brother of Jesus and James. Also, the short but powerful apologetic letter he wrote between AD 70 and 80. Earlier in his life, Jude had rejected Jesus as the divine Messiah (John 7:1-9). But following Jesus' resurrection from the dead, he converted along with his other brothers (Acts 1:14). Jude eventually became a church leader in Jerusalem. He refers to himself as a "slave of Jesus Christ" (Jude 1). His letter vigorously defends Christianity against false Gnostic-like teaching (Jude 5-16), which denied that Jesus was the Son of God and turned Christian liberty into a license to sin.

Judea: the New Testament name for the land of Judah after it became a Roman province (Matthew 2:1,5; 3:1; 4:25; Acts 28:21).

Judges: an anonymous book written between 1043 and 1000 BC. It begins with Joshua's death, ends with the rise of the prophet Samuel (Judges 2:6-9), and focuses on the judges of Israel at that time. The Hebrew title (*Shophet*) can also mean "deliverers" or "saviors." This points to the intended role of these judges. "The LORD raised up judges, who saved them out of the hands of these raiders" (Judges 2:16 NIV).

Judgment of Believers: this phrase is not in the Bible, but it refers to the judgment all Christians will experience when they stand before the judgment seat of Christ (Romans 14:8-12). At that time, each Christian's life will be examined in regard to deeds done while in the body (Psalm 62:12; Ephesians 6:7-8). Personal motives, intents of the heart, and the words we have spoken will also be weighed (Jeremiah 17:10; Matthew 12:35-37; 1 Corinthians 4:5). This judgment has nothing to do with salvation; those who have truly placed faith in Christ are saved, and nothing threatens that. Believers are eternally secure in their salvation. This judgment rather has to do with the reception or loss of rewards.

Judgment of Fallen Angels: an eternal fire that was prepared for the devil and his angels (Matthew 25:41; 2 Peter 2:4; Revelation 20:10). The Bible teaches this doctrine but does not use this phrase.

Judgment of Israel: This takes place after the tribulation period, prior to the millennial kingdom. Those who are recognized as believers in Jesus will be invited into Christ's millennial kingdom (Ezekiel 20:34-38). The Bible teaches this doctrine but does not use this phrase.

Judgment of the Nations: a judgment of Gentiles that takes place after the tribulation period, prior to the millennial kingdom (Matthew 25:31-46). Believers among the Gentiles will be invited into Christ's millennial kingdom, and the others enter into eternal punishment. The Bible teaches this doctrine but does not use this phrase.

Judgment of Unbelievers or the **Great White Throne Judgment** (Revelation 20:11-15): At the end of the millennial kingdom, Christ's 1000-year reign on the earth, He will judge the unsaved dead of all time. Those who face Christ at this judgment will be judged on the basis of their works (Revelation 20:12-13). It is critical to understand that they actually appear at this judgment because they are already unsaved. This judgment will not separate believers from unbelievers, for all who will experience it will have already made the choice during their lifetimes to reject the God of the Bible. Once they are before the divine Judge, they are judged according to their works not only to justify their condemnation but also to determine the degree to which each person should be punished throughout eternity (Luke 12:47-48).

Judgment Seat of Christ (Greek: *bema*): where all believers will one day stand to give an account for their works (Psalm 62:12), their words (Matthew 12:35-37), and even their thoughts (Jeremiah 17:10; 1 Corinthians 4:5; 2 Corinthians 5:10; Revelation 2:23).

Justification: a legal term that has both a negative and a positive nuance. Negatively, the word means that one is once-for-all pronounced not guilty before God. Positively, the word means that man is once-for-all pronounced righteous (Romans 3:25,28,30). This happens at the moment of faith in Christ (Romans 5:1). Though the Jews previously tried to earn right standing with God by works, Paul indicated that God's declaration of righteousness (justification) is given "freely by his grace" (Romans 3:24). The word *grace* means "unmerited favor." Because of God's unmerited favor, human beings can freely be declared righteous before God. This does not mean God's declaration of righteousness has no objective basis, because it does. The word *redemption* literally means "ransom payment." This is a word adapted from the slave market. We were formerly enslaved to sin and Satan, but Jesus ransomed us by His death on the cross. His shed blood was the ransom payment (Romans 3:25). This makes justification possible.

K

Kadesh or **Kadesh-Barnea**: an area southeast of the Dead Sea. This is where the sojourning Israelites initially refused to enter the Promised Land (Genesis 14:7; Numbers 13:3-26; 14:29-33; 20:1; 27:14).

Kenites: a tribe that lived in the desert area between southern Palestine and the mountains of Sinai. This tribe was kind to Israel during Israel's journey to Canaan (Judges 1:16).

King of kings and Lord of lords: a title of Jesus Christ indicating absolute authority and sovereignty over all things (1 Timothy 6:15; Revelation 19:16).

Kingdom of God and **Kingdom of Heaven**: interchangeable terms for God's present spiritual reign over His people (Colossians 1:13) and Jesus' future reign in the millennial kingdom (Revelation 20). This latter kingdom is prophesied many times in the Old Testament (for example, Isaiah 65:17–66:24; Jeremiah 32:36-44; Zechariah 14:9-17).

Kings, 1 and **2**: books written by an unknown author around 550 BC focusing on Israel's division into two kingdoms—the northern kingdom (retaining the name Israel) and the southern kingdom (called Judah). Sadly, the two sets of kings and their kingdoms became indifferent to God's laws (1 Kings 9:3-9; 12:25-33). They were thoroughly disobedient, and this ultimately led to Israel's fall in 722 BC and crushing Babylonian captivity for Judah in 587 BC. The author clearly communicates that this dire situation was a direct result of the peoples' long-term disobedience to God (1 Kings 9:3-9). Even so, God's mercy was always still available if there was repentance.

Kinsman-Redeemer: the closest male blood relative, who was responsible to redeem a family member from slavery or marry his relative's widow (Ruth 4 NIV). Jesus became related to us by blood so He could function as our Kinsman-Redeemer and rescue us from sin (Hebrews 2:14-15).

Korah: a common name most famously used of a Levite who led a rebellion against Moses and Aaron (Numbers 16:8,16).

L

Lake of Fire: the eternal abode of Satan, the antichrist, the false prophet, and unbelievers throughout history (Revelation 19:20; 20:10-15). *See also* Hell.

Lamb: the prescribed sacrifice for each morning and evening (Exodus 29:38-42), the Sabbath day (Numbers 28:9), the Passover (Exodus 12:5), and multiple other feasts (Numbers 29:2; Leviticus 23:18-20; 1 Chronicles 29:21; 2 Chronicles 29:21).

Lamb of God: Jesus Christ, whose sacrificial death on the cross brought salvation to all who believe (Isaiah 53:7; John 1:29,36; 2 Corinthians 5:21; 1 Peter 1:19), just as the Passover Lamb ensured the Israelites would be delivered from the final plague in Egypt. Christ's work of atonement is marvelous indeed, for it makes possible the forgiveness of sins for all who trust in Him for salvation (Hebrews 10:17-18).

Lamech: the fifth in descent from Cain. He feared neither God nor man (Genesis 4:17-18; 5:28-29).

Lamentation: a literary genre that expresses mourning and great sorrow (2 Samuel 1:17-27; Ezekiel 27:2,32; 28:12; 32:2,16; Amos 8:10).

Lamentations: a book written by Jeremiah in about 586 BC that expresses his deep anguish over Judah's sin and the destruction of Jerusalem, the city of God, by the

Babylonians in 587 BC. Jeremiah seems to have witnessed the destruction firsthand. The temple was destroyed, and the people were deported to live in Babylon in exile. This book depicts the funeral of a city and is the only book in the Bible that consists solely of laments.

Laodicea: a wealthy and commercially successful city east of Ephesus and west of Colossae. Jesus warned the church there that it was lethargic and useless—like water that was neither cold enough to drink nor hot enough to bathe in (Revelation 3:15-20).

Laver: the basin priests used to wash their hands and feet before ministry rituals (Exodus 30:18,28; 31:9; 35:16; 38:8; 39:39).

Law: the written code revealing God's will for human conduct, including all the divine commands and precepts regulating man's moral life without and within. The law was given to Israel not to place a burden on the people, but to set them apart and distinguish them from surrounding pagan nations. The law was provided to make the Israelites wise, great, and pleasing to a holy God. Those who obeyed the law reaped great blessing. Those who disobeyed the law brought discipline upon themselves. This is one of the primary emphases of the Sinai covenant (Exodus 19:3-25).

Lazarus: the brother of Mary and Martha in Bethany. Jesus raised him from the dead (John 11:1-44). Also, a poor beggar in one of Jesus' parables (Luke 16:19-31).

Leah: Laban's eldest daughter, who was Rachel's sister and Jacob's wife (Genesis 29:15-30).

Leaven: yeast, which causes dough to ferment and rise (Exodus 12:15,19; 13:7; Leviticus 2:11). Used metaphorically in the New Testament of the kingdom of God (Matthew 13:33), corruption (Matthew 16:6,11-12), and false doctrine (Galatians 5:7-9).

Lebanon: a mountainous region north of Palestine (Joshua 9:1; Judges 3:3).

Legion: a regiment of the Roman army. Metaphorically, a great multitude (Matthew 26:53; Mark 5:9).

Lemuel: a royal author of some of the proverbs (Proverbs 31:1,4).

Leprosy: various infectious skin diseases that were incurable in Bible times. Lepers were banned from contact with other people (Leviticus 13; 14; Numbers 12:10-15).

Levi: Jacob and Leah's third son (Genesis 29:34), and Levi's descendants, who became one of Israel's tribes, and the land they inherited. Also, a name for the apostle Matthew.

Leviathan: an unidentified large animal, perhaps a crocodile or even a marine dinosaur (Job 41:1).

Levirate Marriage: an ancient custom in which a surviving brother married a deceased brother's wife and raised her children, guaranteeing that the deceased brother's family line would continue (Genesis 38:8; Deuteronomy

25:5-10). The practice is recorded in the Bible, but the precise term is not used.

Levite: a descendant of the tribe of Levi (Exodus 6:25; Leviticus 25:32; Numbers 35:2; Joshua 21:3,41). Levites engaged in sanctuary service (1 Kings 8:4; Ezra 2:70).

Leviticus: a book written by Moses between 1445 and 1405 BC. Following the Israelites' exodus from Egypt, they were called to a new way of life, involving priests, tabernacle worship, sacrifices, and the like, and so rules and regulations regarding these matters became necessary. Leviticus contains laws about offerings and sacrifices (Exodus 1–7), laws on the appointment and conduct of priests (8–10), laws about ritual cleansing, personal hygiene, and food (11–15), instructions regarding the Day of Atonement (16), and information and laws regarding Israel's festivals (17–27).

Lo-Ammi (not my people): the symbolic name of Hosea's second son, which represented God's rejection of His sinful, unrepentant people (Hosea 1:9-10).

Lo-Ruhamah (she has not obtained compassion): the name of Hosea's first daughter (Hosea 1:6; 2:23), which warned Israel that they were living outside of God's compassion.

Lois: Timothy's maternal grandmother (2 Timothy 1:5).

Lord of Hosts: God, the sovereign commander of a great army of angels (Psalm 89:6,8; 91:11-12).

Lord (master, ruler): an English translation of the Hebrew words *Yahweh* (printed in capital letters—Genesis 4:3; Exodus 6:3) and *Adonai* (Genesis 18:2; 40:1; Exodus 21:1-6; Joshua 5:14) in the Old Testament, and the Greek word *kurios* in the New Testament (John 20:28; Acts 2:36; Romans 10:9; Philippians 2:11).

Lord's Day: the first day of the week (Sunday), which the early church made the day of worship (Acts 20:7; 1 Corinthians 16:2).

Lord's Prayer: the prayer Christ taught His disciples in the Sermon on the Mount (Matthew 6:9-13).

Lord's Supper: Jesus' last meal with the disciples prior to His crucifixion. He instituted it as a remembrance of His death and the new covenant (Mark 14:12-26; 1 Corinthians 11:20-26). It also serves as a reminder of the basic facts of the Gospel (11:26), our anticipation of the second coming (11:26), and our oneness as the body of Christ (10:17).

Lot: Abraham's nephew (Genesis 11:27). Also, a small stone for casting lots (Numbers 33:54; Jonah 1:7) as well as a person's inheritance (Joshua 15:1; Psalm 125:3; Isaiah 17:4).

Luke: a ministry companion of the apostle Paul. Also, the Gospel he wrote in approximately AD 60 to ensure that the truth would be known about Jesus Christ in a reliable, ordered, and accurate way (Luke 1:1-4). Luke was a doctor, yet he expressed unflinching belief in Jesus' many miracles (4:38-40; 5:15-25; 6:17-19; 7:11-15). Joy is a common theme throughout the book (Luke 1:44,47; 10:21; 15:7,10). Luke is the only New Testament author who was never a Jew. Together, his two books (Luke and Acts) are longer than all of Paul's epistles combined.

Lydia: a woman in Thyatira who lived in Philippi and sold purple cloth. The Lord opened her heart to respond to the apostle Paul's message (Acts 16:13-15).

Lystra: a town of Lycaonia in Asia Minor. When a lame man there was healed, the crowds wanted to worship Barnabas as Zeus and worship Paul as Hermes. But later, Jews incited the crowds to stone Paul and leave him for dead (Acts 14:8-23).

M

Macedonia: a Roman province north of Greece (Acts 16:9). Through a vision, Paul was summoned to preach the gospel there (Acts 18:5; 19:21; Romans 15:26; 2 Corinthians 1:16; 11:9; Philippians 4:15).

Mary Magdalene: a follower of Christ who ministered to Him and witnessed His crucifixion and resurrection (Matthew 27:50-56; 28:1-8; Mark 15:40). Jesus had cast seven demons out of her (Mark 16:9).

Magic and **Witchcraft**: the attempt to contact the dead or harness the power of a deity (Ezekiel 13:20; Revelation 21:8; 22:15). God condemns all forms of occultism, including magic and witchcraft (Exodus 22:18; Leviticus 19:31; Deuteronomy 18:9-13).

Magistrate: a public civil officer (Deuteronomy 1:16-17; Judges 18:7; Luke 12:58; Titus 3:1).

Magog: one of the nations in the end-times northern military coalition that will invade Israel (Ezekiel 38:1-6). It apparently refers to the mountainous area near the Black and Caspian Seas.

Maher-Shalal-Hash-Baz (spoil hastens): the symbolic name of one of Isaiah's sons, referring to the sudden attack on Damascus (capital of the nation of Aram and the chief city in the entire region of Syria) by the army of Assyria (Isaiah 8:1-3).

Malachi (my messenger): an Old Testament postexilic prophet. Also, the book he wrote between 433 and 400 BC. The people had returned to their homeland from exile and rebuilt the temple, but this had not translated into a desire to walk closely with God. They practiced empty rituals without attaching any real meaning to them. Malachi thus spoke forceful and indicting words to move the people to faithfulness to the covenant that God had established with them. If they continued to live like they were, more judgment was surely on the horizon. Repentance was therefore in order!

Mammon: wealth or riches (Luke 16:9-11 KJV, NKJV).

Mamre: a place near Hebron where Abraham lived and provided hospitality to some angels (Genesis 23:17-19; 35:27).

Manasseh: Joseph's first son, born in Egypt (Genesis 41:51; 48:1). Also, Manasseh's descendants, who became one of Israel's tribes, and the land they inherited (Numbers 1:10,35; 2:20-21).

Manna (what is it?): food that God supernaturally provided to the Israelites during the wilderness wanderings (Exodus 16:15-35; Numbers 11:7; Deuteronomy 8:3,16).

Mantle: a cloak worn over other clothing (1 Kings 19:13,19; 2 Kings 2:8,13).

Marah (bitter): an oasis with a spring or well of water so bitter that the Israelites could not drink from it (Exodus 15:23-24; Numbers 33:8).

Maranatha (our Lord, come): an Aramaic term of devotion (1 Corinthians 16:22).

Mark: a coworker of the apostle Paul. Also, the Gospel he wrote between AD 50 and 60. This is the shortest of the four Gospels and was probably the earliest one written. Mark is certainly the most fast paced and action packed of the four. It is bustling with life and action. Indeed, scholars have noted that this Gospel focuses on Jesus' actions (especially His miracles) more than His teachings. It demonstrates that Jesus is who He claimed to be—the divine Son of God. About one-third of Mark's Gospel focuses on the last week of Jesus' life on earth, concluding with His death and resurrection.

Mars' Hill: a rocky hill in Athens where the apostle Paul reasoned with pagan philosophers and defended the truth of Christianity (Acts 17:22-31 KJV).

Martha: a resident of Bethany, where she lived with her sister, Mary, and her brother, Lazarus (Luke 10:38-41; John 11:1-39). These three were close friends of Jesus.

Martyr: a person who bears witness to the truth and suffers death in the cause of Christ (Acts 22:20; Revelation 2:13; 17:6 KJV).

Mary: the name of several women in the New Testament, including Jesus' mother and disciple, who was a "bond-slave of the Lord" (Luke 1:38), a humble servant of God. Mary was truly a godly woman. Her scriptural literacy is evident in the Magnificat (Luke 1:46-55). She was also blessed among women (Luke 1:42,48). This blessedness was due not to something intrinsically within her, but was rather related to what God Himself chose to do by allowing her to give birth to the Messiah.

Matthew: a tax collector, also known as Levi, who became one of the 12 apostles. Also, the Gospel he wrote between AD 50 and 60, prior to the destruction of the Jewish temple by the Romans. Matthew was a Jew, writing to convince Jews that Jesus is the promised Messiah (Matthew 2:17-18; 4:13-15; 13:35; 21:4-5; 27:9-10). His Gospel contains about 130 Old Testament citations and allusions, more than any other Gospel (for example, 2:17-18; 4:13-16; 13:35; 21:4-5; 27:9-10). Matthew's genealogy of Jesus is particularly relevant in this regard. Since Matthew's Gospel was written to Jews, he needed to prove to Jews that Jesus was the fulfillment of the Abrahamic covenant (Genesis 12:1-3) and the Davidic covenant (2 Samuel 7:12-14), so he traces Jesus' lineage to Abraham and David.

Matthias: the man chosen to replace Judas Iscariot (Acts 1:23,26).

Media: a country near Assyria, Armenia, and Persia. The Medes and Persians formed the Medo-Persian Empire and replaced Babylon as a world power, as the prophet Daniel had predicted (Daniel 5:31; 11:1).

Mediator: an intermediary. Jesus is our perfect Mediator, representing God to man (because He is God) and man to God (because He is also a man) (1 Timothy 2:5).

Meditation: objective contemplation and deep reflection on God's Word (Joshua 1:8), His attributes, and His works (Psalm 119).

Megiddo: a Canaanite city that Joshua conquered during the conquest (Joshua 12:21).

Melchizedek: a historical person who prophetically

foreshadowed Jesus Christ as a righteous king-priest (Genesis 14:18).

Mene, Mene, Tekel, Upharsin (numbered, numbered, weighed, and divided): a strange phrase indicating that God intended to put an end to the Babylonian kingdom (Daniel 5:25-28). Its supernatural transcription on a wall is the source of the common expression, "The writing is on the wall."

Mephibosheth: a son of Jonathan who had crippled feet (2 Samuel 4:4; 19:26). David showed grace to him by restoring his inheritance (2 Samuel 9).

Mercy Seat: the lid of the ark of the covenant, which signified the place of atonement (Leviticus 16:15).

Meribah: a fountain in the Desert of Sin where Moses disobeyed God by striking the rock twice instead of speaking to it, as God instructed, to provide water for the Israelites (Exodus 17:1-7; Numbers 20:9-13).

Meshach: the title given to Mishael, one of the three Hebrew youths who were thrown into a fiery furnace for refusing to worship a Babylonian idol (Daniel 1:7; 2:49; 3:12-30).

Meshech and Tubal: two nations in a northern military end-times coalition that will invade Israel (Ezekiel 38:1-6). These refer to the geographical territory to the south of the Black and Caspian Seas.

Mesopotamia: a territory east of Canaan bounded by the Euphrates and Tigris Rivers (Genesis 24:10; Deuteronomy 23:4; Judges 3:8,10).

Messiah (anointed one): the Old Testament parallel to the New Testament term *Christ* (Greek: *christos*) (Luke 2:11,26). That the terms are equated is clear from John 1:41 (NIV), quoting and clarifying Andrew: "'We have found the Messiah' (that is, the Christ)." Hundreds of messianic prophecies in the Old Testament point to Jesus as the Messiah or the Christ (Isaiah 7:14; 9:1-7; 11:2-5; 52:13–53:12).

Methuselah: the son of Enoch and grandfather of Noah. He lived longer than any other person in the Bible (Genesis 5:21-27; 1 Chronicles 1:3).

Micah: an Old Testament prophet and the book he wrote in approximately 700 BC. Micah was a simple farmer whose prophetic message targeted the injustices and exploitation he had witnessed. His primary message was that those who were rightly related to God should be interested in social justice and reach out to help the poor and disenchanted. But instead of this, those who claimed to be right with God in his day continued to ignore social injustices and exploit the poor. Micah indicted Samaria and Jerusalem as well as the leaders and people of Israel and Judah. He insisted that God hates injustice. God's desire for people is "to act justly and to love mercy and to walk humbly with your God" (Micah 6:8 NIV).

Micaiah: the name of a number of Old Testament persons, including a faithful prophet of Samaria (1 Kings 22:8-28).

Michael the Archangel: the top ranking angel (Daniel 10:13; Jude 9). *See also* Archangel.

Michal: the younger of Saul's two daughters. She married David (1 Samuel 14:49-50; 18:20-28).

Midian: the fourth son of Abraham by Keturah (Genesis 25:2; 1 Chronicles 1:32). Also, his descendants, who inhabited the desert north of the peninsula of Arabia (Genesis 37:36; Numbers 31:2).

Midtribulationism: the view that Christ will rapture the church in the middle of the tribulation, based largely on the theory that the two witnesses of Revelation 11 (who are caught up to heaven in the middle of the tribulation) are representative of the church. This term is not in the Bible.

Millennial Kingdom: the 1000-year kingdom Christ will set up on earth following His second coming (Revelation 20:2-7). This term is not in the Bible.

Miriam: the sister of Moses and Aaron (Exodus 2:4-10; 1 Chronicles 6:3).

Mishael: one of the three Hebrew youths who were trained in Babylon (Daniel 1:11,19). God miraculously delivered them when they were thrown into a fiery furnace for their refusal to engage in idolatrous worship.

Moab: the eldest son of Lot and brother of Ammon (Genesis 19:37). Also, the nation of his descendants and the land they inhabited (Jeremiah 48:24).

Molech: a detestable Ammonite god that was worshipped by the sacrifice of children (Leviticus 18:21; 1 Kings 11:7).

Money Changers: individuals who converted foreign currency into the local currency, often charging an exorbitant fee in the process (see Matthew 21:12).

Mordecai: a Jew who exposed Haman's plan to exterminate the Jews (Esther 2:21; 3:8-15; 6:2–7:10; 9:26-32).

Moriah: the mountain Abraham ascended to offer his son Isaac in sacrifice (Genesis 22:2).

Moses: a Hebrew, the son of Amram and Jochebed, and the brother of Aaron and Miriam (Exodus 6:20; Numbers 26:59). He was raised in Egyptian royalty and was "educated in all the wisdom of the Egyptians and was powerful in speech and action" (Acts 7:22 NIV). God, through the hand of Moses, worked ten mighty miraculous judgments against prideful Pharaoh and the Egyptians, and the Israelites were eventually released from enslavement (Exodus 5–11). At Mount Sinai, God delivered to Moses the Ten Commandments to govern the lives of the people. God also provided instructions for the building of the tabernacle. It was at Mount Sinai that the Israelites finally became a nation, and the laws delivered to them through

Moses constituted God's covenant stipulations, which He expected them to obey (Exodus 19–20).

Mount of Megiddo: a location about 60 miles north of Jerusalem where several Old Testament battles took place. This will also be the site of the final horrific battles of humankind just prior to the second coming, associated with Armageddon (Revelation 16:16).

Mount of Olives: a high hill to the east of Jerusalem that derived its name from the dense olive groves that covered it. It is where Jesus prayed before the crucifixion (Matthew 26:39), where He ascended to heaven (Luke 24:50-51; Acts 1:12), and where He will return at the second coming (Zechariah 14:4).

Myrrh: an aromatic resin used as an ingredient in anointing oil (Exodus 30:23), as a burial spice (John 19:39), and as a perfume (Esther 2:12; Psalm 45:8; Proverbs 7:17).

Mystery: a truth unknown to people living in Old Testament times but revealed to humankind by God in New Testament times (Matthew 13:17; Colossians 1:26).

N

Naaman: the name of several biblical persons, including a Syrian commander with leprosy who was healed by following Elisha's strange instructions (2 Kings 5; Luke 4:27).

Nahum: an Old Testament prophet and the book he wrote in approximately 650 BC. This book predicts the fall and destruction of Nineveh, the Assyrian capital, in graphic language. About a hundred years previously, the Ninevites had repented under the preaching of Jonah. But now Nineveh had returned in full force to idolatry, paganism, and brutality (Nahum 3:1-4). Nahum thus prophesied that even though the Assyrians might seem invincible, their days were numbered, for judgment was rapidly approaching. Nineveh is pictured as a prostitute that had hurt others and that must now be punished. Just as Nahum prophesied, Assyria was utterly destroyed in 612 BC.

Naomi: the mother-in-law of Ruth and Orpah (Ruth 1:2,20-21; 2:1).

Naphtali: Jacob's sixth son (his second with Bilhah, Rachel's servant). Also, Naphtali's descendants, who became one of Israel's tribes, and the land they inherited.

Nathan: the name of several biblical persons, including a prophet during the reigns of David and Solomon (2 Chronicles 9:29).

Nazarene: a term ascribed to Jesus, perhaps because He was raised in Nazareth (Matthew 2:23; Luke 4:16).

Nazareth: Joseph and Mary's humble hometown in Galilee, situated among the southern ridges of Lebanon, about fourteen miles from the Sea of Galilee and about six miles west of Mount Tabor. This is the city where the angel Gabriel announced the birth of the Messiah to Mary (Luke 1:26-28) and where Mary and Joseph raised Jesus (Luke 2:39; 4:16; John 1:45).

Nazarite: a person who is specially consecrated to God. Nazarites didn't drink wine or strong drink, cut their hair, or go near dead bodies (Numbers 6:1-21).

Nebo: a term used variously in Scripture for a pagan Chaldean god (Isaiah 46:1; Jeremiah 48:1) and a mountain in the land of Moab from which Moses saw the Promised Land (Deuteronomy 32:49; 34:1).

Nebuchadnezzar: the most powerful of the Babylonian kings. He took multitudes of Jews into captivity in 586 BC, including Daniel and his companions (Daniel 1:1-2; Jeremiah 27:19; 40:1).

Nehemiah: an Old Testament governor who led a group of Jewish exiles back to Jerusalem and who oversaw the rebuilding of the city wall and the renewal of the people's spiritual lives. Also, the book he wrote between 445 and 425 BC.

Nephilim: giants, mighty men, or men of great stature (Genesis 6:4; Numbers 13:33).

Nethinim: temple servants (Ezra 2:70; 7:7, 24; 8:20 NKJV).

New Covenant: an unconditional covenant God made

with humankind in which He promised to provide for forgiveness of sin, based entirely on the sacrificial death and resurrection of Jesus Christ (Jeremiah 31:31-34).

New Heaven and New Earth: the renovated cosmos God will create as the eternal habitation for all believers (Matthew 19:28; Acts 3:21; Revelation 21:1-5). The eternal city, known as the New Jerusalem, will rest upon the new earth.

New Jerusalem: the heavenly city designed for the habitation of Christians in the eternal state, measuring approximately 1500 by 1500 miles (Revelation 21; 22:1-5). As we read John's description of the New Jerusalem, we find many contrasts with the present earth. Earthly cities are dark at night, but the New Jerusalem is always lighted (Revelation 22:5). Earthly cities succumb to disease, but healing characterizes the New Jerusalem (22:2). Earthly cities suffer drought, but the river of life will flow forever (22:1-2).

New Moon: a holy day on which sacrifices atoned for defilements related to the temple and holy food (Numbers 10:10 NIV; 28:11-15 NIV).

New Testament: a collection of 27 books and epistles composed over a 50-year period by several different authors, all writing under the inspiration of the Holy Spirit. The primary personality of the New Testament is Jesus Christ. The primary theme is salvation in Him, based on the new covenant, which makes full provision for the forgiveness of sins (Luke 22:20; 1 Corinthians 11:25). The first four books of the New Testament are the Gospels: Matthew, Mark, Luke, and John. Each of these contains an account of the life of Christ. Following the Gospels is the book of Acts, which focuses on the spread of Christianity following Jesus' ascension. Following the book of Acts are the epistles or letters. The apostle Paul wrote 13 of these, and the rest were written by James, Peter, Jude, and John (the book of Hebrews is anonymous). Most of Paul's epistles are responses to churches' particular questions and problems. The final book of the New Testament is the book of Revelation, which is an apocalyptic book full of prophecy.

Nicodemus: a Pharisee and member of the Sanhedrin who believed in Jesus Christ (John 3:1-21).

Nicolaitans: a corrupt, pleasure-loving group who ignored moral law and promoted license in Christian conduct (Revelation 2:6,15).

Nicolas: one of seven original deacons in the early church (Acts 6:5).

Nile: the most important river in Egypt, which the Egyptians worshipped as a god called Nilus. The true God, through Moses, showed that He alone is God when He turned the Nile into blood (Exodus 1:22; 7:20).

Nimrod: a descendant of Cush who had a reputation as a mighty hunter (Genesis 10:9).

Nineveh: the capital of Assyria (2 Kings 19:36; Isaiah 37:37).

Noah: the famous patriarch and grandson of Methuselah who built the ark at God's instruction to rescue his family and the animals. He was a just man who walked with God (Genesis 5:25-29; 6:14-16).

Numbers: a book written by Moses between 1445 and 1405 BC that derives its name from the two censuses (numberings) that are recorded in the book—one at Mount Sinai (the original Exodus generation) and one on the plains of Moab (the generation that grew up in the wilderness and conquered Canaan). Aside from these censuses, the book also contains a listing of the tribes of Israel (Numbers 2), regulations for the priests and the Levites (3–8), information about the Passover (9), a chronicle of Israel moving from Mount Sinai to Moab on the border of Canaan (10–21), a record of Balaam and Balak (22–32), and the Israelites' journey coming to an end (33–36).

O

Obadiah: an Old Testament prophet and the book he wrote between 848 and 841 BC. Obadiah ministered during King Johoram's reign in Judah and predicted the downfall of Edom, an area directly southeast of the Dead

Sea that is rich in mountainous terrain. The Edomites had invaded Judah when Jerusalem was being overrun and destroyed by the Babylonians in 587 BC. Obadiah indicated that the Edomites would be destroyed, but the Israelites would one day be restored to their land.

Offering: something a person gives to God or dedicates to Him in order to please Him (Genesis 4:3-4).

Ointment: a salve used for medicinal purposes (Exodus 30:25; Psalm 133:2; Isaiah 1:6; Amos 6:6; John 12:3; Revelation 18:13).

Old Gate: a gate on the north wall of Jerusalem (Nehemiah 3:6; 12:39).

Old Testament: a collection of 39 books, written under the inspiration of the Holy Spirit, that document the old covenant between God and the Israelites, according to which the Jews were to be God's people and were to be obedient to Him, and God would bless them (Exodus 19:3-25). The Old Testament contains the Law, the Prophets, and the Writings. The Law is also called the Torah, the first five books of the Old Testament, written by Moses—Genesis, Exodus, Leviticus, Numbers, and Deuteronomy. The Prophets contains 21 books, including such notables as Isaiah, Ezekiel, and Jeremiah. The Writings make up the rest of the Old Testament books, including such notables as Psalms, Proverbs, and Job.

Interestingly, in Luke 24:44 Jesus said the entire Old

Testament referred to Him—including the Law, the Prophets, and the Psalms (a term used apparently in reference to the Writings).

Olivet Discourse: the prophetic teaching Jesus delivered from the Mount of Olives (Matthew 24:3).

Omega: the last letter in the Greek alphabet (Revelation 1:8). It is joined with *Alpha* in a New Testament title for Jesus Christ (21:6).

Onesimus: Philemon's runaway slave. After Onesimus met Paul and converted to Christ, Paul sent him back to Philemon with a letter asking Philemon to forgive Onesimus and receive him as a brother (Colossians 4:9; Philemon 1:10).

Onyx: a precious stone included on the breastplate of the high priest and the shoulders of the ephod (Exodus 28:9-12,20; 35:27; Job 28:16; Ezekiel 28:13).

Orpah: a daughter-in-law of Naomi (Ruth 1:4,14).

=== **P**

Palestine (land of Philistines): the region south and southwest of the Lebanon ranges, northeast of Egypt, and north of the Sinai Peninsula (Joel 3:4 KJV). The term came to refer to the land of the Hebrews. It was also called the holy land (Zechariah 2:12), the land of promise (Hebrews 11:9, because it had been promised to Abraham—Genesis 12:7; 24:7), the land of Canaan (Genesis 12:5), the land of Israel (1 Samuel 13:19), and the land of Judah (Isaiah 19:17).

Parable (place alongside): a teaching tool Jesus often used, citing everyday stories to illustrate spiritual truths. Jesus drew from family life (Luke 15:11-32), agriculture (Matthew 13:1-9), shepherding (John 10:1-16), business (Matthew 20:1-16), and more.

Paradise of God: heaven (2 Corinthians 12:4; Revelation 2:7).

Paran: the wilderness territory in the central part of the Sinai Peninsula. Moses sent the 12 spies from Paran to investigate Canaan (Genesis 21:21; Numbers 13:3,26).

Partial Rapture: This term is not in the Bible. It describes the view that the only Christians who will be raptured are those who are faithful and watchful. Unfaithful Christians will be left behind to suffer through the tribulation (Matthew 25:1-13).

Passover: a festival that celebrates the Israelites' escape from Egypt under Moses' leadership (Exodus 12:3-11). More specifically, it commemorates God's instruction (through Moses) for the Israelites to smear the blood of a lamb on their doorposts so God would "pass over" their houses when He destroyed all the firstborn of Egypt (Exodus 12:13).

Patmos: a mountainous, rocky desert island of about 60 square miles in the Aegean Sea, off the southwest coast of

Asia Minor. On this desolate and barren island, the aged apostle John received the sweeping vision recorded in the book of Revelation (Revelation 1:9).

Patriarchs: the leaders of Israel preceding the time of Moses, including Abraham, Isaac, Jacob, and Jacob's sons. Abraham was the most important patriarch. His name means "father of a multitude," and he lived around 2000 BC.

Paul: a Pharisee (Philippians 3:5). Though born and raised in Tarsus in Cilicia (a Gentile city—Acts 22:3), he studied in Jerusalem under Gamaliel, one of the outstanding Jewish rabbis of the day (Acts 5:34). Paul was known as a brilliant student (Galatians 1:14). Following his conversion to Christianity (Acts 9), his background as a Jew put him in a unique position to be able to explain how Jesus and Christianity fulfilled the Old Testament Scriptures. He went on three missionary tours, preaching primarily to Gentiles, and wrote more than half the books in the New Testament.

Peace Offering: a gift that expresses the desire to maintain right relations between God, man, and neighbor (Deuteronomy 12:18; 16:11; Judges 20:26; 21:4).

Pentateuch (five books): the first five books of the Bible—Genesis, Exodus, Leviticus, Numbers, and Deuteronomy, all written by Moses.

Pentecost (50): the feast of harvest (Exodus 23:16), elsewhere called the feast of weeks (Exodus 34:22) because it was held seven weeks (or 50 days) after the feast of unleavened bread. On the day of Pentecost, the Holy Spirit was poured on the disciples, tongues of fire rested on their heads, and they spoke in other languages (Acts 2).

Penuel: a place near where Jacob wrestled all night with the angel of the Lord (Genesis 32:24-32).

Pergamum: a city in northwest Asia Minor (modern-day Turkey) and the site of one of the seven churches mentioned in Revelation 2–3. In Revelation 2:12-17 the risen Christ commended the church for maintaining its faith, but He also chastened it, urging members to stand against the teaching of Balaam.

Persia: one of the nations in the end-times northern military coalition that will invade Israel (Ezekiel 38:1-6). Persia is modern-day Iran.

Peter, 1 and **2**: epistles written AD 63 to 65 by Peter, one of Jesus' three closest disciples, who saw some of His greatest miracles (Mark 9; 2 Peter 1:16-18). Peter wrote 1 Peter to encourage and strengthen believers in facing persecution under Nero. Peter may well have recalled his Lord's injunctions: "Strengthen your brothers" (Luke 22:32) and "Feed my sheep" (John 21:15-17 NIV, KJV, NKJV). In 2 Peter, the apostle addressed errors regarding morality and Christ's return.

Pharaoh: the official title of ancient Egypt's kings (Genesis 12:10-20; Exodus 1:8-22).

Pharisees: a religious and political party in Palestine

during New Testament times that sought to preserve and obey the Mosaic Law and encouraged other people to do the same. The word *Pharisee* comes from an Aramaic word meaning "separated"; Pharisees were "the separated ones." They placed extreme emphasis on the Sabbath, tithing, and ritual purity (Matthew 23:23-26; Mark 2:24; 7:1-13; Luke 11:37-42).

Philadelphia: a city in Lydia, located in western Asia Minor, or modern-day Turkey. The church in this city was faithful to Christ (Revelation 1:11).

Philemon: a Christian slave owner, leader of the church at Colossae, and friend of the apostle Paul. Also, the letter Paul wrote to him in approximately AD 63, regarding Onesimus, Philemon's slave. Onesimus had stolen some money and escaped. He later met Paul, became a Christian, and returned to Philemon with Paul's letter urging Philemon to receive Onesimus as a brother in Christ so he could return to help Paul in his work of ministry.

Philip: the name of several New Testament men, including one of the twelve apostles (John 1:44), one of the seven original deacons (Acts 6:5), and the tetrarch of Ituraea (Luke 3:1).

Philippians: a letter written by Paul in AD 63. Philippi, in northern Greece, about ten miles inland from the Gangites River, was named after Philip II of Macedon. Paul wrote his letter to the church primarily to address such

problems as intense rivalries (Philippians 2:3-4), distur-
bances caused by Judaizers (3:1-3), and libertinism (3:18-
19). Paul also wrote this letter to thank the Philippians for
their support to his ministry (Philippians 1:3).

Philistines: inhabitants of Philistia, located directly to the
southwest of Canaan. This pagan nation often opposed
the Israelites. They worshiped numerous pagan deities
(Judges 16:23; 1 Samuel 5:1-7; 2 Kings 1:2).

Phoenicia: a coastal land north of Israel (Acts 21:2).

Phylacteries: small square leather cases containing Scriptures written on parchment. Devout Jews wore them on
their foreheads (Exodus 13:1-10; Deuteronomy 6:4-9;
11:18-21; Matthew 23:5).

Pilate: *see* Pontius Pilate.

Pithom: an Egyptian storage city built by Hebrew slaves
(Exodus 1:11).

Polygamy: the marrying of multiple wives (Deuteronomy 17:17). Monogamy is God's design (1 Corinthians
7:2; 1 Timothy 3:2,12).

Polytheism: the belief in many gods, each thought to have
control over some part of nature, such as the sky, or land,
or sea. The Bible consistently affirms only one God (Isaiah 44:6).

Pontius Pilate: the Roman governor of Judea who presided at Jesus' trial and ultimately ordered His crucifixion
(Matthew 27:2,11-26).

Pontus: a large Roman province in northern Asia Minor (Acts 2:9; 18:2).

Postmillennialism: the view that through the church's progressive influence, the world will be Christianized before Christ returns. In postmillennialism, the millennium will basically involve a thousand years of peace and prosperity that precedes Christ's physical return. This word is not in the Bible.

Posttribulationism: the view that Christ will rapture the church after the tribulation at the second coming of Christ. This means the church will go through the time of judgment prophesied in the book of Revelation, but believers will allegedly be "kept through" Satan's wrath during the tribulation (Revelation 3:10). This word is not in the Bible.

Potiphar: the Egyptian official in Pharaoh's government who purchased Joseph as a slave from Midianite traders (Genesis 37:36).

Potsherd: a fragment of pottery (Job 2:8). Potsherds were sometimes used to write on.

Potter's Field: a piece of land that Jewish leaders purchased with Judas' blood money (Matthew 27:7-10).

Praetorian: a Roman imperial bodyguard (Philippians 1:13).

Prayer: communication with God involving thanksgiving,

praise, worship, confession, and specific requests (Psalm 34:1; 95:2; 100:4; Proverbs 28:13; Matthew 6:9-13; 7:7-8; Ephesians 5:20; Philippians 4:6-7; Colossians 3:15; 1 Thessalonians 5:17; 1 John 5:14). Scripture teaches much about prayer. All our prayers are subject to the sovereign will of God (1 John 5:14). Prayer should not be an occasional practice but rather a continual practice (1 Thessalonians 5:17). Sin is a hindrance to answered prayer (Psalm 66:18). Living righteously, on the other hand, is a great benefit to answered prayer (Proverbs 15:29). The Lord's Prayer is a good model (Matthew 6:9-13). We should be persistent in praying (Matthew 7:7-8). We should pray in faith (Mark 11:22-24). We should pray in Jesus' name (John 14:13-14).

Predestination: God's choice of certain people—those whom He foreknew—to come to saving faith in Christ (Romans 8:28-30).

Prefect: a Persian government official (Jeremiah 51:23; Daniel 3:3).

Premillennialism: the teaching that following the second coming, Christ will institute a kingdom of perfect peace and righteousness on earth that will last for 1000 years (Revelation 20:1-6). This word is not in the Bible.

Pretribulationism: the view that Christ will rapture the entire church before any part of the tribulation begins. This means the church will not go through the judgments prophesied in the book of Revelation (1 Thessalonians 1:9-10; 5:4-9; Revelation 4–18). This word is not in the Bible.

Prewrath Rapture: the view that the rapture occurs toward the end of the tribulation but before the great wrath of God falls—between the sixth and seventh seals (Revelation 6:12–8:1). This term is not in the Bible.

Priests: official worship leaders and ministers who represented the people before God and who were in charge of various rituals and offerings prescribed by God (Exodus 20:26; Leviticus 10:8-11; 16:4,23-25; 21:1-15; 22:1-9).

Prince: a governor (1 Kings 20:14 KJV) or satrap (Esther 3:12).

Priscilla: the wife of Aquila (Acts 18:2).

Promised Land: the land of Canaan, described figuratively as flowing with milk and honey, that was promised to the descendants of Abraham as an everlasting possession (Genesis 17:8).

Prophecy: God's revelation about future events (Isaiah 46:9-11).

Prophet: a person who spoke God's words to the people, sometimes predicting the future and other times declaring God's view of current circumstances and events.

Propitiation: the full satisfaction of God's holy demands against sinful human beings that was provided by Jesus' sacrificial death on the cross (Romans 3:25; Hebrews 2:17; 1 John 2:2; 4:10).

Proselyte: a new convert. Specifically in the New Testament, a Gentile who converts to Judaism (Acts 2:10; 6:5).

Proverbs (to be like, to be compared with): a collection of maxims of moral wisdom completed by 700 BC. Solomon wrote many of them (1 Kings 4:32). They use comparisons or figures of speech to crystallize and condense the writers' experiences and observations about life in order to help the young in ancient Israel acquire mental skills that promote wise living.

Providence: God's preservation and governing of all things. The word is used once (Job 10:12 NIV), but the concept is common in Scripture (Colossians 1:17; Hebrews 1:3).

Psalms: a compilation of five smaller collections or books: Book 1 (Psalms 1–41) contains primarily personal psalms relating to David. Books 2 and 3 (Psalms 42–72 and 73–89) are primarily national psalms, some of them written after the nation was divided into the northern kingdom and the southern kingdom. Books 4 and 5 (Psalms 90–106 and 107–150) are primarily worship psalms. The psalms were written from about 1410 to 450 BC.

The psalms were collected for use in temple worship and were often set to the accompaniment of stringed instruments. They include prayers, poetic expressions, liturgies, hymns, and just about every emotion known to man, including happiness, serenity, peace, hatred, vengeance, bitterness, and much more. In the psalms, we find human beings struggling honestly with life and communicating honestly with God without holding anything back. Because we today struggle with the same kinds of problems and emotions that the ancients did, the book of Psalms is one of the most relevant and loved books to modern Christians in the entire Bible. The psalms are indeed timeless.

Publican: a tax collector (Matthew 10:3 KJV).

Purification: cleansing procedures required by the Old Testament law to rid people of defilement (John 2:6).

Purim: a feast instituted by Mordecai in memory of the deliverance of Persian Jews from the murderous plot of Haman (Esther 9:24-32).

Put: one of the nations in the end-times northern military coalition that will invade Israel (Ezekiel 38:5), probably modern-day Libya.

_____ **R**

Rabbi or **Rabboni** (teacher or master): a respectful Jewish title, often used of Christ (Matthew 23:6-8; Mark 10:51; John 1:38,49; 3:2; 6:25; 20:16).

Raca (empty head): a term of derision (Matthew 5:22 KJV, NKJV, NIV).

Rachel: the second wife of Jacob and the mother of Joseph and Benjamin (Genesis 29:6,28; 30:22-24).

Rahab: a prostitute in Jericho who helped two of the twelve Israelite spies (Joshua 6:17-25).

Rameses: an Egyptian storage city built by Hebrew slaves (Exodus 1:11).

Ramoth-Gilead: a city of refuge on the east side of the Jordan River (Deuteronomy 4:43; Joshua 20:8; 21:38).

Ransom: the payment for a life (Exodus 21:30). Used figuratively of nations who suffered so Israel could be blessed (Isaiah 43:3) and of Jesus' death for the redemption of humankind (Matthew 20:28).

Rapture: that glorious event in which the dead in Christ will be resurrected, living Christians will be instantly translated into their resurrection bodies, and both groups will be caught up to meet Christ in the air (1 Thessalonians 4:13-17) and taken to heaven (John 14:1-3; 1 Corinthians 15:51-54; 1 Thessalonians 4:13-17). This means there will be one generation of Christians who will never pass through death's door.

Rebekah: the wife of Isaac and mother of Esau and Jacob (Genesis 22:23; 24:67).

Reconciliation: the removal of the alienation and

estrangement between parties and the restoration of their relationship. The New Testament emphasizes the reconciliation of the world to God as a result of the forgiveness of sin (2 Corinthians 5:19).

Red Sea: a narrow body of water that moves southeast from Suez to the Gulf of Aden for 1300 miles (Exodus 14–15; Numbers 33:8; Deuteronomy 11:4).

Redeemer: one who buys back or purchases something. Jesus Christ purchased us from the slave market of sin (Romans 3:24; 8:23; Ephesians 1:7; Colossians 1:14). The payment price was His own blood (Mark 10:45).

Redemption: buying back or purchasing something. Christ paid the ransom price of His own blood to purchase us from the slave market of sin (Matthew 20:28; Mark 10:45).

Regeneration: the spiritual rebirth people experience when the Holy Spirit gives them new life (John 3:5; 2 Corinthians 5:17; Titus 3:5).

Rehoboam: the son and successor of King Solomon (1 Kings 11:43; 12:16-18).

Repentance (to change one's mind): a religious or ethical change in the way a person thinks and acts, particularly in regard to the issues of sin and righteousness (Matthew 4:17; Luke 1:16; 24:47; Acts 3:19; 9:35; 11:21; 14:15; 15:19; 26:18-21; 1 Thessalonians 1:9; 1 Peter 2:25). In some biblical examples, the change of mind had to do not with sin but with the identity of Jesus, as is apparently the case with the Jews who had rejected Jesus as the divine Messiah (Acts 2:38).

Rephaim: giants, perhaps referring to descendants of the Nephilim (Genesis 14:5; 2 Samuel 21:16,18).

Resurrection: the restoration of a dead person to life. Jesus was physically and bodily resurrected from the dead (Luke 24:39; John 2:19-21). Luke begins his second volume by affirming, "After [Jesus'] suffering, he showed himself to [the apostles] and gave many convincing proofs that he was alive. He appeared to them over a period of forty days and spoke about the kingdom of God" (Acts 1:3 NIV). Paul also provided evidence for the resurrection: "[Jesus] appeared to more than five hundred of the brothers at the same time, most of whom are still living" (1 Corinthians 15:6 NIV). *See also* First Resurrection and Second Resurrection.

Reuben: Jacob's first son (Genesis 29:32). Also, Reuben's descendants, who became one of Israel's tribes, and the land they inherited.

Revelation: God's self-disclosure to human beings. Also, an apocalyptic New Testament book written by the apostle John in approximately AD 95 while exiled on the isle of Patmos. Topics include the exalted Jesus (chapter 1), letters to the seven churches of Asia Minor (2–3), the tribulation (4–18), the second coming (19), the millennial kingdom

(20), and the eternal state (21–22). The recipients of the book of Revelation were undergoing severe persecution, and some of them were killed (Revelation 2:13). Things were about to get even worse. John wrote this book to give his readers a strong hope that would help them patiently endure in the midst of suffering. By showing them the future, John revealed that in the end, we win!

Rewards: crowns that believers will receive or lose at the judgment seat of Christ, depending on how they lived on earth (Romans 14:8-10; 1 Corinthians 3:1-10; 9:25; 2 Corinthians 5:10).

River of Life: an apparently real and material river in the New Jerusalem that is also symbolic of the perpetual flow of spiritual blessing from the throne of God to the redeemed of all ages (Revelation 22:1-2).

Romans: a letter Paul wrote in approximately AD 57. Paul discusses humankind's sin problem and the universal need for righteousness (Romans 1:18–3:20), salvation and justification by faith (3:21–5:21), freedom from the power of sin and domination of the Law (6:1–8:39), the Jews' unique place in God's plan (9:1–11:12), spiritual gifts (12:3-8), submission to the government (13:1-7), and unity between Jews and Gentiles (15:5-13). These broad theological themes make this letter immensely practical for the Christian life.

Rome: the capital city of the Roman Empire. It was

founded in 753 BC about 15 miles from where the Tiber River flows into the Mediterranean Sea. A trade center of the ancient world, it featured large buildings and impressive architecture. It was characterized by moral degradation, paganism, and emperor worship.

Rosh: apparently a reference to Russia. This will be one of the nations that will invade Israel in the end times (Ezekiel 38:2; 39:1).

Rulers: an order of angels that participate in God's heavenly government (Colossians 1:16).

Ruth: a Moabite widow. Also, a book written during the time of the judges in about 1000 BC, perhaps by the prophet Samuel, though this is uncertain. The book focuses on Naomi and her Moabite daughter-in-law, Ruth, and God's providential provision for them (Ruth 1:6-18).

S

Sabaoth (hosts): the starry universe (Genesis 2:1). Also, the heavenly army (Joshua 5:13-15). God is the Lord of hosts (Romans 9:29 ESV; James 5:4).

Sabbath: the Jews' holy day of rest for man and animals (Exodus 20:8-11). The origins of the Sabbath are in the creation account. This day was to commemorate God's rest after His work of creation (Genesis 2:2). God set the pattern for living—working six days and resting on the seventh.

Sabbatical Year: a stipulation in the Law of Moses to let the land remain uncultivated every seventh year (Leviticus 25:2-7).

Sabeans: descendants of Seba in southwest Arabia (Genesis 10:7).

Sackcloth: a coarse cloth made of black goat hair that was used for sacks but also worn by mourners (Genesis 37:34; 42:25; 2 Samuel 3:31; Esther 4:1-2; Psalm 30:11).

Sacraments: a thirteenth-century word (not in the Bible) for two New Testament rituals—the Lord's Supper and baptism—that celebrate Jesus' death and resurrection, the new covenant, and the believer's identification with Christ (Matthew 28:19; Romans 6:1-4; 1 Corinthians 11:20-30).

Sadducees: a Jewish sect that believed only in the Torah and denied the existence of angels, the resurrection, and the immortality of the soul (Matthew 22:23-33; Acts 4:1-3; 5:17-18).

Salem: Jerusalem (Genesis 14:18; Psalm 76:2; Hebrews 7:1-2).

Salt Sea: the Dead Sea (Joshua 3:16).

Salvation: a past, present, and future redemption. In the past, God delivered believers from the penalty of sin and wiped their slate clean. This happened the moment they trusted in Christ for salvation (Acts 16:31). In the present, God delivers believers from the power of sin in their daily lives (Romans 8:13; Philippians 2:12). In the future, when Christians enter into glory, God will deliver them from the presence of sin (Romans 13:11; Titus 2:12-13).

To describe the wonder and all-encompassing nature of believers' new status in Christ, Scripture says they are born again (John 3:1-5; 1 Peter 1:23), justified (Romans 3:24), reconciled (2 Corinthians 5:19), forgiven (Hebrews 10:17), and adopted (Romans 8:15).

Samaritans: inhabitants of Samaria, a territory in central Canaan. They were considered racially unclean by the Jews (John 4:9).

Samson: the son of Manoah who was set apart for God's service by a Nazirite vow (Judges 13:5; 16:17). He is famous for his incredible strength, which, amazingly, was related to the length of his hair (15:15).

Samuel, 1 and **2**: books written by a prophet of the same name sometime after 931 BC. The two books chronicle Israel's history from the time of the judges through the reign of King David, who reigned from 1011 to 971 BC—about 135 years of history. During this time, Israel demanded a king like the nations around them, and Samuel anointed the first king, Saul, who reigned from 1052 to 1011 BC. These books, then, chronicle the transition in Israel's leadership from judges to kings.

Sanctification: setting apart a person or thing to make it holy (Exodus 13:2; 40:10-13; Romans 12:1-2; 1 Corinthians 6:11; 1 Peter 3:15).

Sanctuary: a place of worship such as the tabernacle (Exodus 25:8; Leviticus 12:4; 21:12) or the temple (1 Chronicles 22:19; 2 Chronicles 29:21).

Sanhedrin: the Jews' supreme ruling and administrative council. It included scribes, elders, chief priests, and the high priest (see the NIV in Matthew 5:22; 26:59; Mark 15:1).

Sapphira: wife of Ananias (Acts 5:1-11). *See also* Ananias.

Sapphire: a precious stone associated with diamonds (Exodus 28:18) and emeralds (Ezekiel 28:13).

Sarah: the wife and half-sister of Abraham and the mother of Isaac (Genesis 11:29; 20:12).

Sardis: one of the seven churches of Asia Minor mentioned in Revelation 2–3 (see Revelation 3:1-6). The city is about 30 miles southeast of Thyatira. Jesus had stern words for this church: "You have the reputation of being alive, but you are dead" (3:1 NIV).

Sargon: an Assyrian king who succeeded Shalmaneser V. He ruled from 722–705 BC and was the father of Sennacherib (Isaiah 20:1).

Satan: a fallen angel, formerly known as Lucifer, who is aligned against God and His purposes. He leads a vast company of fallen angels, called demons, who are also aligned against God and His purposes. He is the ruler of this world (John 12:31), the god of this world (2 Corinthians 4:4), and the prince of the power of the air (Ephesians 2:2), and he deceives the whole world (Revelation 12:9; 20:3). He is also called the accuser of the brethren (Revelation 12:10), our adversary (1 Peter 5:8), the devil (Matthew 4:1), our enemy (Matthew 13:39), the evil one (1 John 5:19), the father of lies (John 8:44), a murderer (John 8:44), a roaring lion (1 Peter 5:8-9), the tempter (Matthew 4:3), and a serpent (Genesis 3:1; Revelation 12:9).

Saul: Israel's first king, who was appointed by the prophet Samuel (1 Samuel 10–11). Also, the apostle Paul's Hebrew name (Acts 13:9).

Savior: the divine Messiah, who brings salvation to His people (Isaiah 43:11; Luke 2:11; John 4:42; Titus 2:13).

Scapegoat: On the Day of Atonement, the high priest laid his hands on this goat and symbolically transferred the guilt of the nation to it. He then sent the scapegoat into the wilderness, symbolizing atonement (Leviticus 16:26).

Scepter: a staff that symbolized authority (Genesis 49:10; Numbers 24:17; Psalm 45:6; Isaiah 14:5).

Scourge: a whip (John 2:15). Also, to flog (Matthew 27:26).

Scribes: copyists, editors, and teachers of the law (Matthew 22:35; Luke 7:30). Jesus warned of their hypocrisy (Matthew 23).

Sea of Galilee: a freshwater lake fed by the Jordan River. Several of Jesus' disciples fished in this lake. This is where Jesus walked on the water and calmed a storm (Matthew 4:18,22; 15:29; Mark 1:16-20; 7:31). It is also called the lake of Gennesaret (Luke 5:1-11).

Second Coming: This phrase isn't in the Bible, but describes a real event. Jesus Christ will return to earth in great glory at the end of the present age. When He returns as the King of kings and Lord of lords, He will set up His kingdom (Matthew 24:29-30; Acts 1:7; 1 Timothy 6:14; 1 Peter 4:13; Revelation 1:7; 19).

Second Resurrection: the restoration of life to unbelievers who have died (John 5:29; Revelation 20:11-15). This occurs after the millennial kingdom and leads to judgment. *See also* First Resurrection.

Seer: a prophet, especially one who sees visions (1 Samuel 9:9; 2 Samuel 15:27; 24:11; 1 Chronicles 9:22; 25:5; 2 Chronicles 9:29; Amos 7:12; Micah 3:7).

Selah: a pause or interlude in the reading of a psalm (Psalm 3:2,4,8).

Sennacherib: an Assyrian king (705–681 BC.) noted for his military campaigns against Judah, the southern kingdom (2 Kings 18:13; 19:16,20).

Sepulchre (KJV) or **Sepulcher (NKJV)**: a tomb or burial cave (Genesis 23:6 KJV; Isaiah 22:16 NKJV).

Seraphim: glorious angels who are burning in their devotion to God and who hover about God's throne proclaiming His holiness (Isaiah 6:1-6).

Sermon on the Mount: one of five major discourses of Christ recorded in the Gospel of Matthew (Matthew 5:1). In this sermon, Jesus spoke of the blessed rewards of living as God desires (5:3-12), the necessity of Christians being like salt and light in our fallen world (5:13-16), the need for true righteousness (5:17-48), avoiding hypocrisy (6:1-18), putting the kingdom of God first (6:19-34), avoiding judging others (7:1-6), praying rightly (7:7-12), choosing the "narrow way" (7:13-14), bearing fruit (7:15-20), and doing good deeds (7:21-29). This sermon presents the highest standard of Christian living.

Serpent: in the Bible, often a personification of evil (Genesis 3:1; 2 Corinthians 11:3; Revelation 12:9; 20:2).

Seth: the third son of Adam and Eve (Genesis 4:25; 5:3).

Shadrach: a Chaldean name given to Hananiah, one of the Jewish youths exiled in Babylon in 605 BC (Daniel 1:7; 3:12-30).

Shear-Jashub (a remnant shall return): the symbolic name of one of Isaiah's sons that emphasized Isaiah's prophecy that a remnant would return to the land after a time of captivity (Isaiah 7:3; 10:21-22).

Sheba: an ancient country in south Arabia, whose queen visited King Solomon to observe his wisdom (2 Chronicles 9:1). Also, the name of several other biblical persons.

Shechem: an ancient fortified city in the central part of Canaan that was the first capital of the northern kingdom, Israel (Genesis 12:6; 33:18; 1 Kings 12:1).

Shekel: a unit of weight amounting to about a half ounce. Also, a silver coin (Exodus 30:13; Matthew 17:27).

Shem: a son of Noah (Genesis 5:32; 6:10) and the ancestor of the Semites.

Shema: an early Hebrew confession of faith that begins, "Hear, O Israel: The LORD our God, the LORD is one" (NIV). The entire Shema can be found in Numbers 15:37-41 and Deuteronomy 6:4-9; 11:13-21. Also, the name of several little-known people in the Bible.

Sheol: an Old Testament word often used for hell. Sheol is full of horror (Psalm 30:9), weeping (Isaiah 38:3), and punishment (Job 24:19).

Shibboleth: a password (or a test word) used by the Gileadites at the Jordan River to identify the fleeing Ephraimites, who could not pronounce the word correctly (Judges 12:6).

Shiloh: a city in Ephraim that was an Israelite religious center during the time of Joshua and later (Joshua 18:1; Judges 18:31).

Shinar: an ancient Babylonian plain where the tower of Babel was built (Genesis 10:10; 11:1-6).

Shofar: a ram's horn, blown like a trumpet as a signal to Israel (Psalm 81:3).

Showbread: consecrated unleavened bread placed on a table in the sanctuary every Sabbath (1 Chronicles 28:16; 2 Chronicles 13:11).

Sickle: a metal utensil with a wooden handle used for reaping grain (Jeremiah 50:16), sometimes symbolizing divine judgment (Revelation 14:15).

Signet: a ring that leaves an impression on wax or clay, designed to seal edicts and other documents (Daniel 6:8-10,12).

Simeon: Jacob's second son (Genesis 29:33); Simeon's descendants, who became one of Israel's tribes; and the land they inherited. Also, an aged man who visited the temple when the infant Jesus was being presented before the Lord (Luke 2:29-35).

Simon: the name of several people in the New Testament, including one of the 12 apostles (Matthew 10:4; Mark 3:18), the father of Judas Iscariot (John 6:71; 13:2,26), a half brother of the Lord (Matthew 13:55; Mark 6:3), a Pharisee (Luke 7:36-38,40), a leper of Bethany (Matthew 26:6-13; Mark 14:3-9), a Jew of Cyrene (Matthew 27:32), a sorcerer (Acts 8:9-11), a Christian at Joppa (Acts 9:43), and Simon Peter (Matthew 4:18).

Sin (to miss the target): a failure to live up to God's perfect standards. All of us miss the target. No one is capable of fulfilling all of God's laws at all times (Romans 3:23). Some people may be more righteous than others, but all of us fall short of God's infinitely perfect standards. None of us can measure up to His perfection.

Sin Offering: a sacrifice presented for ritual cleansing, often at Hebrew festivals, or for forgiveness of unintentional sins against God (Leviticus 4:5-13).

Sinai: a peninsula where the Israelites wandered through the wilderness. Also, the mountain on that peninsula on which Moses received the Law from God (Exodus 19:11; 31:18; 34:29).

Sinai Covenant: Though this phrase isn't in the Bible, it describes the covenant God made with the Israelites at Mount Sinai after delivering them from Egypt. It constituted the formal basis of His relationship with them (Exodus 19:3-25).

Smyrna: the home of one of the seven churches mentioned in Revelation 2–3, located about 35 miles north of Ephesus. Christ admonished the Christians in this pagan city to be faithful until death, and they would receive a crown of life (Revelation 2:10).

Sodom: a city at the southern end of the Dead Sea that God destroyed because of its wickedness (Genesis 10:19; Romans 9:29).

Sodomite: a person guilty of unnatural sexual acts (Deuteronomy 23:17 KJV).

Solomon: David's son and successor, who became king in 970 BC when he was about 20 years old (1 Kings 11:42). Solomon was best known for his unparalleled wisdom (1 Kings 3; 4:29-34). He wrote the majority of the book of Proverbs and spoke some 3000 proverbs during his lifetime. Nonetheless, he eventually strayed from God's commands, and the kingdom suffered as a result (1 Kings 11).

Son of God: a title of Jesus Christ, the second person of the Trinity. Among the ancients, the phrase *son of* often signified an equality of being. When Jesus claimed to be the Son of God, His Jewish contemporaries fully understood that He was claiming to be God (John 19:7).

Son of Man: a messianic title (Daniel 7:13) often used of Christ in the New Testament (Matthew 8:20; 20:18; 24:30).

Song of Solomon: an extended poem written by Solomon shortly after 971 BC (1 Kings 4:32). It is full of metaphors and imagery describing the richness of sexual love between husband and wife (see Song of Solomon 1:8–2:7). The backdrop, of course, is that God Himself created male and female as sexual beings (Genesis 1:28). Therefore, sex within the boundaries of marriage is God-ordained and is to be enjoyed (Genesis 2:24; Matthew 19:5; 1 Corinthians 6:16; Ephesians 5:31). Any deep relationship brings both joy and pain, and the Song of Solomon reflects this, pointing to both the joys and heartaches of wedded love (Song of Solomon 5:2–7:9).

Soothsayer: a person who uses magic to foretell the future (Joshua 13:22 NKJV).

Sorcery: the magical use of potions to control the world of nature (Galatians 5:20; Revelation 18:23; 21:8; 22:15).

Soul: a living being (Genesis 2:7), the seat of the emotions and experience (Psalm 13:2), or man's immaterial nature (Genesis 35:18). The New Testament sometimes uses the words *soul* and *spirit* interchangeably (Luke 23:46; Acts 7:59; Philippians 1:21-23; 2 Corinthians 5:6-8).

Speaking in Tongues: the Spirit-given ability to speak in languages not known to the speaker. This phenomenon occurred on the Day of Pentecost (Acts 2) and several other occasions in the book of Acts (10:44-48; 11:13-18; 19:1-7).

Spirit: a word that can refer to the immaterial nature of human beings (Acts 7:59; 1 Corinthians 5:5; 7:34), angels (good and bad—Luke 4:36; Hebrews 1:14), or the Holy Spirit (Ephesians 4:30).

Spirit of Antichrist: a spirit that is already at work in the world promoting heretical doctrine (1 John 4:1-3; 2 John 7). *See also* Antichrist.

Spiritism: the attempt to consult with the dead (Deuteronomy 18:10-11).

Stephen: one of the seven original deacons and the first Christian martyr (Acts 6:7–7:60).

Stoics: Greek philosophers who taught that people should be free from all passion, unmoved by either joy or grief (Acts 17:18).

Surety: something of worth given to secure a pledge; collateral (Proverbs 22:26).

Synagogue: a place of worship for Jewish congregations. Synagogues first emerged when Israel was in captivity in Babylon.

Syria: a nation northeast of Palestine. Also called Aram (2 Samuel 8:6 NKJV, 17:23; Matthew 4:24; Acts 15:23,41; 20:3).

T

Tabernacle: the heart and center of Israelite religious life during the wilderness wandering (Leviticus 26:11). It was where sacrifices were offered to God. It featured two rooms: the holy place, which only priests could enter, and the holy of holies, where the presence of God dwelt (Exodus 26:33) and where only the high priest could enter on the Day of Atonement.

Tabitha: a disciple at Joppa known for her almsgiving. Peter raised her from the dead (Acts 9:36-43).

Table of Showbread: a table upon which 12 loaves of bread were presented by the 12 tribes of Israel on each Sabbath as a meal offering to God (Leviticus 24:5-9).

Talent: a Hebrew measure of weight amounting to 75 pounds (Matthew 18:24; 25:15).

Tammuz: a Mesopotamian sun god (Ezekiel 8:14).

Tares: weeds (Matthew 13:25-30).

Tarsus: a city in the southeast part of Asia Minor that was the capital of Cilicia and was the native home of the apostle Paul (Acts 21:39).

Tartarus: the Greek word translated *hell* in 2 Peter 2:4.

Tekoa: a city south of Bethlehem that was the birthplace of Amos (Amos 1:1).

Temple: the center of Israelite worship for approximately 1000 years. Solomon, the son of David, built the first temple (1 Kings 6–7; 2 Chronicles 3–4). The holy place (the main outer room) housed the golden incense altar, the table of showbread, and five pairs of lampstands. Double doors led into the holy of holies, which contained the ark of the covenant. This temple was destroyed by Nebuchadnezzar and the Babylonians in 587 BC. After the Babylonian exile, the Jews finished building a smaller temple in 515 BC. It lasted 500 years. Herod the Great completed a third temple in AD 64. It was much larger and more resplendent than Solomon's temple. Titus destroyed it and the rest of Jerusalem in AD 70.

Ten Commandments: the commandments God gave to Moses on tablets of stone at Sinai (Exodus 20:2-17). The first four pertain to the Israelites' relationship with God, and the remaining six deal with their relationships with each other. These commandments were not just religious rules, but governed the whole of life. The tablets on which the commandments were inscribed were put in the ark of the covenant (Deuteronomy 10:5; 1 Kings 8:9).

Terah: the father of Abraham, Nahor, and Haran (Genesis 11:24-32; Joshua 24:2).

Teraphim: household idols or gods in a human shape that were supposed to bring prosperity (2 Kings 23:24; Zechariah 10:2).

Testament: a covenant or formal agreement (Hebrews 9:15 KJV).

Tetrarch: a Roman ruler of a province (Matthew 14:1; Acts 13:1).

Thaddaeus: one of the 12 apostles (Mark 3:18).

Theophilus: a Christian to whom Luke dedicated both his Gospel and the book of Acts (Luke 1:3; Acts 1:1).

Thessalonians, 1 and **2:** epistles written by Paul to the church at Thessalonica in AD 51 to answer some of the questions the new believers there had about spiritual matters and to correct a few wrong ideas. For example, Paul had already taught them that Jesus would one day come again. But what about Christians who died before Christ came? Some of the Thessalonian Christians were very concerned about this, so Paul wrote 1 Thessalonians to assure them that the dead in Christ will indeed rise from the dead (1 Thessalonians 4:13-17). Several months later, he wrote 2 Thessalonians to further explain and clarify God's program of events relating to the day of the Lord (including Christ's second coming).

Thomas: one of the 12 apostles (Matthew 10:3; Mark 3:18). He is widely known as "doubting Thomas" for his initial skepticism about Christ's resurrection (John 20:24-28).

Thorn in the Flesh: the apostle Paul's physical affliction that kept him dependent on the grace of God (2 Corinthians 12:7-10).

Throne of David: the throne mentioned in the Davidic covenant (2 Samuel 7:11-16; 1 Chronicles 17:10-14). A descendant of David (Jesus Christ) will rule on this throne for 1000 years during the future millennial kingdom (Matthew 1:1; Luke 1:32-33).

Thummim: an item in the high priest's breastplate. Somehow, God revealed His will through the Urim and Thummim (Exodus 28:30; Leviticus 8:8).

Thyatira: a city in Asia Minor located about halfway between Pergamum and Sardis (Acts 16:14). Christ commended the church in this city for its love, faith, service, and endurance (Revelation 2:19), but He also chastised it for tolerating the woman Jezebel (verses 21-23).

Tiberias: a city on the Sea of Galilee built in honor of the Roman emperor Tiberius (John 6:23).

Timothy, 1 and **2:** pastoral epistles that the apostle Paul wrote in AD 62–64 to his young and trusted colleague, Timothy (Acts 17:4,15; 1 Corinthians 4:17). Paul provided practical advice on false doctrine (1 Timothy 1:3-7; 4:1-3), disorder in worship (1 Timothy 2:1-15), qualifications for church leaders (1 Timothy 3:1-14), and faithfulness in the work of ministry (2 Timothy 1:6,13-14; 3:15–4:5).

Tithe: a tenth of one's income or acquired belongings. Israelites offered tithes to God (Malachi 3:8-10; *see also* 1 Corinthians 16:1-2; Ephesians 4:28).

Titus: a pastoral epistle the apostle Paul wrote in AD 62–64 to Titus, a person in Paul's trusted inner circle (2 Corinthians 8:23). Paul warned against false teachers and urged Titus and his congregation to pursue sound doctrine and good works.

Topaz: a precious stone on the breastplate of the high priest (see Exodus 28:17; Ezekiel 28:13).

Torah: the first five books of the Bible: Genesis, Exodus, Leviticus, Numbers, and Deuteronomy.

Transfiguration: that event when Christ, while still on earth, revealed His divine glory in all its splendor. He was transfigured before the disciples (Matthew 17:2; Luke 9:29).

Treaties: agreements between nations (1 Samuel 11:1; 27:1-12; 1 Kings 5:1-12), between individual people (Genesis 21:22-34; 31:43-55), between individual tribes of Israel (Judges 4:10; 6:35), between friends (1 Samuel 18:3-4), and between God and His people (Exodus 19–20).

Tree of Life: a tree in the Garden of Eden that bestows continuing life (Genesis 2:9,17; 3:1-24). It appears again in the eternal city, the New Jerusalem (Revelation 22:2).

Tribulation: a seven-year period at the end of the age but before Christ's second coming. It will be characterized by great travail (Daniel 9:24,27; Matthew 24:29-35). It will be of such severity that no period in history, past or future, will equal it (Matthew 24:21). It will be characterized by wrath (Revelation 6:16-17), judgment (Revelation 14:7), trouble (Jeremiah 30:7), destruction (Joel 1:15), darkness (Amos 5:18), and desolation (Daniel 9:27).

Trinity: This word is not in the Bible, but it describes the biblical teaching that while there is only one God, there are three coequal and coeternal persons—Father, Son, and Holy Spirit—within the unity of the godhead, each equal in the divine nature but distinct in personhood (Matthew 28:19; 2 Corinthians 13:14).

Tubal: one of the nations that will participate in the end-times invasion into Israel (Ezekiel 38:1-6), probably the geographical territory to the south of the Black and Caspian Seas.

Twelve Tribes of Israel: the 12 tribes that descended from the 12 sons of Jacob (Genesis 49:28) and comprised the nation of Israel. Different portions of the land of Canaan—the Promised Land flowing with milk and honey—were given to each tribe. Reuben, Gad, and half the tribe of Manasseh, settled in the east, while Asher, Naphtali, Zebulon, Issachar, Ephraim, and the other half-tribe of Manasseh settled in the northwest. Benjamin, Judah, Simeon, and Dan settled in the southwest.

Tyre: an ancient Phoenician city that was rich in commerce (Joshua 19:29; Ezekiel 27:3).

U

Unclean: ritually defiled. Foods, utensils, persons, animals, or other items could become unclean (Leviticus 5:2; Psalm 106:39).

Unleavened Bread: bread made from unfermented dough (Genesis 19:3; Exodus 12:15; Matthew 26:17). Passover was also called the Feast of Unleavened Bread.

Ur: an ancient Mesopotamian city near the mouth of the Euphrates (Genesis 11:28; Nehemiah 9:7).

Uriah: a Hittite man married to Bathsheba. David committed adultery with Bathsheba and had Uriah killed (2 Samuel 11:3; 12:9).

==**V**

Vagabond: a wanderer (see the KJV in Genesis 4:12; Psalm 109:10; Acts 19:13).

Valley of Salt: a valley south of the Dead Sea where David defeated the Syrians (2 Samuel 8:13).

Vashti: the Persian queen whom Ahasuerus deposed after she refused to obey his summons to appear in the banquet hall (Esther 1:10-12).

Virgin Birth: this phrase isn't in the Bible, but it describes the biblical teaching that Christ was miraculously conceived in Mary's womb when the Holy Spirit overshadowed her (Matthew 1:18,20-25; Luke 1:26-38). This doctrine explains how the eternal Son of God entered human existence. The divine nature of the eternal Son of God was joined, within Mary's womb, with a human nature by a direct supernatural act of God.

Vision: experiences similar to dreams through which God

reveals supernatural insight or awareness (1 Kings 22:17; Isaiah 6:1-5).

Vow: a solemn and voluntary promise to God to engage in an act or service or perhaps to abstain from something. Once the vow was made, it was to be kept (Genesis 28:18-22; Leviticus 7:16; Numbers 30:2-13; Deuteronomy 23:21).

W

Watch: one of the four-hour time divisions between sunset and sunrise (2 Samuel 18:24-27; 2 Kings 9:17-20; Isaiah 21:5-9).

Winepress: a vat containing grapes where they were trodden upon (Isaiah 16:10; Lamentations 1:15; Joel 3:13). Also, a vat that caught the juice from the previous vat (Nehemiah 13:15; Job 24:11; Isaiah 63:2-3; Joel 2:24; Haggai 2:16).

Wineskin: a pouch made from animal skin that held and dispensed wine (Psalm 119:83).

Winnow: to throw grain against the wind so the chaff will blow away and the seed will fall to the floor (Ruth 3:2; Isaiah 30:24; Jeremiah 4:11-12; Matthew 3:12).

Wise Men: magi—experts in the study of the stars (Matthew 2:1-2).

Witchcraft: an occultic means of extracting information or guidance from a dead person or a pagan god (Numbers 22:7; 23:23; Joshua 13:22).

Witness: one who testifies about what he or she has seen. Criminal cases required more than one witness (Deuteronomy 17:6; 19:15).

Woe: impending doom, grief, or sorrow. Isaiah used the word 22 times, most often in the context of the approaching captivity. Jesus pronounced woes on the scribes and Pharisees (Luke 11:42-44).

Word (Greek: *logos*): a title of Jesus Christ that highlights His role as revealer of God (John 1:1; Revelation 19:13). The Word became flesh (John 1:14) to declare or make known God the Father to humankind (John 1:18).

Wormwood: a star (or more likely a large meteor or an asteroid) that will fall from heaven and cause a deep impact on earth during the future tribulation period (Revelation 8:10-12).

Worship: to bow down or to prostrate oneself (Genesis 22:5; 42:6; Matthew 2:2,8,11). Worship involves reverencing God, adoring Him, praising Him, venerating Him, and paying homage to Him, not just externally (with rituals and songs) but in our hearts as well (1 Samuel 15:22-23; Isaiah 29:13). God alone is to be worshipped (Matthew 4:10; Acts 14:11-18; Revelation 19:10). Worship of Jesus is a testimony of His divinity (Matthew 2:11; 8:2; 9:18).

Wrath of God: God's holy anger as a result of a violation of His holiness. The effects of God's wrath may include affliction (Psalm 88:7), drought (Deuteronomy 11:17), leprosy (Numbers 12:10), pestilence (Ezekiel 14:19), plagues (2 Samuel 24:1), slaughter (Ezekiel 9:8), destruction (Ezekiel 5:15), military defeat (2 Chronicles 28:9), and exile (2 Kings 23:26-27; Ezekiel 19:12).

Y

Yahweh: The eternal, self-existent God. Yahweh never came into being at a point in time, for He has always existed. To know Yahweh is to know the eternal one (Exodus 3:14-15). The name also conveys God's covenant faithfulness to His people.

Yahweh-Nissi (the Lord our banner): God. Israel could not defeat her enemies in her own strength. The battles were to be the Lord's because He was Israel's banner—her source of victory (Exodus 17:15).

Yoke: a wooden bar fitted to the necks of oxen so they could pull a cart or a plough (Numbers 19:2; Deuteronomy 21:3). Metaphorically, a union between people (2 Corinthians 6:14 NIV) or the believer's submission to Jesus Christ (Matthew 11:29).

Zaccheus: a tax collector who followed Jesus (Luke 19:1-10).

Zacharias: a temple priest who was the father of John the Baptist. Because of his initial unbelief regarding the angel Gabriel's message to him of John's impending birth, he was struck dumb until the child was born (Luke 1:12-20,60-80).

Zadok: the name of several biblical personalities, including a high priest during the time of David and Solomon (2 Samuel 20:25; 1 Kings 4:4).

Zealots: fanatical Jewish patriots who believed the Jews should not be subject to any foreign power, such as the Romans (Matthew 10:4). Jesus included a Zealot (Simon) and a tax collector (Matthew) in his original 12 disciples.

Zebedee: a fisherman in Galilee who was the father of the apostles James and John (Matthew 4:21; 27:56; Mark 15:40).

Zechariah: the son of Jeroboam II (king of Israel), who succeeded to the throne for only six months, being murdered by Shallum, who himself then took the throne (2 Kings 14:29; 15:8-12). Also, an Old Testament prophet and the book he wrote between 520 and 518 BC. The book emphasizes the blessing God sought to bestow upon the Jews because He remembered the covenant He made with

Abraham (Genesis 12:1-3). The Jews rejoiced to be restored from their exile, but they were also despondent because their city was ruined—and as a result of their own unfaithfulness at that. Zechariah, along with Haggai, motivated the people to finish the temple so worship could begin again.

Zedekiah: the last king of Judah (2 Kings 23:31; 24:17-18).

Zephaniah: an Old Testament prophet and the book he wrote in approximately 625 BC. His message was that God would judge the Jewish people for not being faithful to the covenant He had established with them. They would be held responsible for following the habits of the pagan cultures around them. Judgment was imminent (Zephaniah 1:2-3; 2:2; 3:6-7).

Zerubbabel: a descendant of the royal line of David who returned to Israel with the exiles from Babylon and helped rebuild the Jewish temple (Ezra 2:64; 3:8-13).

Zilpah: a handmaiden of Leah and a concubine of Jacob. She gave birth to Gad and Asher (Genesis 30:9-13).

Zion: the city of God (Psalm 46:4), God's resting place (Psalm 132:13-14), God's holy hill (Psalm 2:6), the holy city (Isaiah 48:2), and the holy mountain (Daniel 11:45). The term came to refer to the city of Jerusalem as a whole.

Zipporah: the daughter of Jethro and wife of Moses (Exodus 2:21).

Zophar: one of Job's well-meaning but misguided friends who tried to console him during his time of trial (Job 2:11).

Christianity According to the Bible

*The Complete Guide to
Christian Denominations*

Conviction Without Compromise

*Find It Quick Handbook
on Cults and New Religions*

*The Truth Behind Ghosts, Mediums,
and Psychic Phenomena*

*Why Do Bad Things Happen
If God Is Good?*

The Wonder of Heaven

The 10 Most Important Things Series

*The 10 Most Important Things
You Can Say to a Catholic*

*The 10 Most Important Things
You Can Say to a Jehovah's Witness*

*The 10 Most Important Things
You Can Say to a Mason*

*The 10 Most Important Things
You Can Say to a Mormon*

*The 10 Things You Need
to Know About Islam*

*The 10 Things You Should Know
About the Creation vs. Evolution Debate*